चि न्म य   ग्र न्थ   मा ला

KINDLE LIFE

SWAMI CHINMAYANANDA

Central Chinmaya Mission Trust

•

Printed upto December 2002 - 30000 copies
Reprint from December 2003 - January 2006 - 10000 copies
Revised Edition January 2008 - 2000 copies
Reprint from August 2008 - February 2012 - 15000 copies
Reprint March 2013 - 5000 copies

•

Published by:
Central Chinmaya Mission Trust
Sandeepany Sadhanalaya
Saki Vihar Road, Mumbai 400072, India
Tel.: +91-22-2857 2367, 2857 5806, Fax: +91-22-2857 3065
Email: ccmtpublications@chinmayamission.com
Website: www.chinmayamission.com

•

Distribution Centre in USA:
Chinmaya Mission West
Publications Division
560 Bridgetown Pike, Langhorne, PA 19053, USA
Tel.: (215) 396-0390 Fax: (215) 396-9710
Email: publications@chinmayamission.org
Website: www.chinmayapublications.org

•

Printed by:
Parksons Graphics,
Andheri, Mumbai

•

Price: ₹ 135/–

•

ISBN: 978-81-7597-189-9

CONTENTS

S.No.	Topic	Page No.

Publisher's Note

The place of Kindle Life in Chinmaya Study curriculum is very special as it is read by maximum number of people. Youngsters and old people alike use it to understand the basics of Vedānta. Perhaps, many are inspired into spiritual life after reading this preliminary work. Its simplicity of language and easy to read organization make even a beginner very comfortable while reading it. Pujya Gurudev has made important concepts of Vedānta very clear in this textbook for their application in real life.

Pujya Gurudev guides us in this book, chapter by chapter, to live a life of higher values of Truth, Non-violence and Self-control in a very logical fashion. All misunderstanding about the place of religion in our life and the debate regarding rituals and philosophy are resolved in very lucid manner. The reader is introduced to time-tested spiritual practices like the Gāyatrī japa in this invaluable book of our time.

This new edition of Kindle Life is thoroughly revised by incorporating diacritical marks and correcting errors that had unfortunately, crept in earlier editions. We are thankful to Shri Sudhakarji, Rindaniji and Pradeepji for their efforts in bringing out an improved version of Kindle Life.

We hope maximum people will take the benefit of this beautiful work of Pujya Swami Chinmayanandaji and kindle their lives.

Date: **CENTRAL CHINMAYA MISSION TRUST**
01/01/2010   **MUMBAI**

1. FREEDOM AND LICENCE

Man has made this world a glorious place to live in. The phenomenal powers, which have been threatening and persecuting mankind all along, have been tamed and harnessed to serve him. The land, which was barren or wild, has been prepared to yield an abundance of food. People have grown from a primitive and barbarous state to be a civilized and intelligent society. The comforts and amenities provided are almost heavenly and man has been indulging in them without the least restraint. However, sitting amidst a mountain of wealth and prosperity, man lives a life of worry, anxiety and dissatisfaction.

This sad paradox has been the subject of investigation by the spiritual masters who dedicated their lives for the general welfare of mankind. In their subtle enquiries they discovered that uncontrolled and excessive indulgence in sensual enjoyments causes dissipation of one's personality and leads to sorrow and misery. For example, the first helping of a sweetmeat is delicious to eat; the second and the third have a diminishing value, while the twentieth is not only sickening, but also detrimental to one's health.

1

Hence, our ancient benefactors formulated certain basic regulations of self-restraint and discipline for gaining a more permanent joy out of our relationship with the world of objects.

But the essential nature of man being absolute Freedom, he detests any shackles being put on him. He does not relish being told what to do or what not to do. To him, injunctions and precepts are like a red rag to a bull; therefore, he revolts against the idea of any spiritual practice of self-denial.

Little does he realize that freedom is essentially built on intelligent self-restraint and discipline. For instance, the traffic lights on our roads are undoubtedly a restraint laid down by the government on our freedom; but such restraint alone lends a meaning to the freedom of movement and checks its degradation into licentiousness.

This inability to distinguish between freedom and license is at the root of the modern man's aversion to religion. The religious textbooks provide us with the material for a subjective scientific analysis, by which we can intelligently understand and appreciate the necessity for such voluntary self-restraint. They serve the same purpose as manuals supplied with a machine for its efficient use. Similarly, the human machine, the most complex entity in nature, also needs certain adjustments and tuning up according to the manuals of religion, so that, it may function efficiently in all its contacts with the world of things and beings. Man is given the liberty, either to eke out the maximum happiness for him, by following these instructions and harnessing his equipment, or to disregard them, inviting sorrow and suffering for himself. His alone is the choice to make or mar himself and his happiness.

Thus, the scriptural books provide an exhaustive science of better living and, in our maturity; we find in them a complete technique of self-development, culminating in the experience of the supreme Reality. In our attempt to develop ourselves to the stature of a well integrated nation, why should we not bring this proved and well tested method into use?

2. ART OF RIGHT CONTACT

Licentiousness is not true freedom but leads only to one result – disaster. When freedom is punctuated by adherence to the laws of nature and recognition of the rights of others, we grow into the ampler field of peace and prosperity. The constitution of our country recognizes and establishes freedom, but at the same time, it contains a host of rules and regulations restraining us from doing all that we would like to do. These rules and regulations alone lend a meaning to freedom.

Similarly, the religious textbooks, prescribe certain laws of living which define for us the modes of contact with the world of objects around us, so that we may have a more harmonious existence. When there is an intelligent appreciation and faithful adherence to these laws, we maintain the right contact with the world and that alone can bring about a healthy life of dynamic existence. This is best illustrated if we take the example of electricity from practical life. One has the freedom to use electricity in one's home in any manner that one chooses. Nevertheless, to establish a correct relationship with it and to benefit by it, one has to religiously follow the laws of electricity or else; the same power can mercilessly destroy one.

The general complaint is that, the world is full of evil and imperfections, disturbances and despairs, and one often wonders how peace and tranquillity could be found in their midst. But there is no need to despair, for we should bear in mind that a rough surface is, as a rule, essential for sharpening any dull instrument. When one knows the art of applying the tool to the grindstone, it is the roughness of the stone that alone sharpens the tool. So too, in life, when we understand the "Art of establishing Right Contact" with the world, we chasten and edify our subjective personality. The evils of the world, therefore, are not great problems and impediments, but man's lack of dexterity in facing the challenges confronting him, is the real problem.

In not recognizing this simple truth, the right perspective of life is lost and humanity perpetually complains of bad times and a bad world. Consider for instance, a glass only half filled with milk. It is viewed differently by different people according to their own emotional and intellectual stature. One looks at the empty upper half and complains that it is not full while another views the bottom portion and freely enjoys it.

When we carefully analyse the attitude of people in general, we find a continuous procession of such unintelligent mourners. A lame man on a wheel chair despairs at the sight of healthy pair of legs walking past him, but the man who can walk, sighs at another, swiftly passing him on a scooter; the man with a scooter again is jealous of the motor car owner and the latter pines away at the thought of having to pay his income tax. Such, indeed, are the sorrows of all, but there is no need to despair, for, the remedy is quite evident.

Let us develop a sense of gratitude to the Lord, by focussing our attention on what we have, which, a good many less fortunate have not, and are yearning for. By refusing to crave for objects, which we do not have, we shall be conserving a lot of mental energy, which alone can give us peace within, and a capacity to act rightly in the world.

3. MAN'S HERITAGE

Independence is the very essence of manhood, and he who has disengaged himself from his slavish dependence upon the world of objects for gaining his flashes of joys, is truly independent. Others are only beings, who, like feathers in the summer breeze, are tossed about hither and thither by the problems and challenges of the world.

The sense objects of the world present to us a false glitter of joy. To resist this call of flesh, the all-consuming onslaught of our senses, is the privilege and glory of man. Such a man of perfection stands out like a lighthouse in the sea of life, graceful and unaffected by the lashes of the turbulent waves. Not knowing this art of independent living, we remain like a neglected boat on the agitated ocean of material changes. To reach the quiet and peaceful harbour of perfection, we will have to follow the technique adopted by a mariner who is lost on the high seas.

Man being essentially divine by nature, the call of the Higher is in the bosom of every one of us, but while facing the challenges of life, we know not the right direction in which to turn. **The scriptures, like a**

7

true compass, always indicate the right direction. And, just as the mariner trusts the accuracy of the compass and moves on, we will have to steer our ship of life with faith in, and devotion to the scriptures, until we attain the higher state of peace and perfection.

A man, who has thus gained mastery over his environment and consequently remains calm and unmoved by them, is generally mistaken to be nothing but an inert statue, which remains unaffected by either a garland, offered round its neck or a crow sitting on its head. There is a general criticism and condemnation of such a man for his state of his apparent indifference and disinterest in the affairs of the world. Such feelings arise out of our ignorance of his supreme achievement; for, it is not true to say that such a man is devoid of emotions. He certainly has them, but does not allow them to overwhelm him. An emotion or sympathy for another is certainly a virtue, but emotionalism ruins one's poise and balance in life, and is an impediment to any progress, either material or spiritual. Sentiments adorn a person, but sentimentalism is an ugly scar on his personality.

The ancient masters of this great country were mighty stalwarts, who stood amidst life's storms as firm as the great Himālayas. Their emotions and sentiments made their hearts bleed for the suffering humanity, but their heads were above the clouds in the ever-peaceful realm of the high ideal.

A man may be tossed about by uncertain storms of life, but the solution to it lies in his own efforts in finding an ideal in life, and then raising his personality from the level of petty emotions to the loftier heights of the chosen ideal. The secret of success in life thus lies in keeping the head above the storms of the heart. A successful man never allows his faculty of discrimination and judgement to be disturbed by the rising tides of his emotions.

Let us be dedicated to an accepted and well tested ideal, and let us develop the courage to live our convictions fully, entirely and wholly. This intellectual honesty, to live true to our conviction in full dedication to the ideal, adds a serene cadence to our individual life. The success and beauty of the individual life help to build the glory and effectiveness of the nation.

4. THE JOY OF LIVING

Man, in his pilgrimage from the womb to the tomb, is incessantly motivated, and propelled by two inevitable impulses, namely, revulsion to sorrow and a craving for joy. He avoids and discards disagreeable things and unconducive environment and runs after the agreeable and the conducive. Thus, as objects and environment keep continuously changing in the world, man engages himself in an endless chase after happiness. The methods employed by different individuals in procuring it may be distinct and varied, but the goal sought after is common to all. It should, therefore, be interesting to analyse and discover where exactly happiness is located.

Our firm belief today is that the joys we experience through our senses lie in the objects of the world. Consistent with this belief, we are constantly engaged in acquiring, possessing and aggrandizing more and more wealth. But a little reflection reveals to us that the acquisition and possession of wealth is no measure of the quantum of one's happiness. We are but too familiar with the striking contradictions in life between a millionaire sitting and mourning in his palatial apartments and an ill-clad peasant, roaring in ecstatic joy amidst his poor circumstances!

Again, if the joy is inherent in the sense objects, then each object should provide the same quantum of joy to all those who come in contact with it. Obviously, this is far from the truth. For instance, a cigarette fills one with joy and satisfaction, while it drives another mad with annoyance. What is the cause for the satisfaction of one and the annoyance of the other? This leads us to the fundamental question – **What is happiness?**

On a careful analysis we find that man's happiness is entirely a subjective phenomenon, for there seems to be a distinct and clear relationship between the state of his mind and the joy or sorrow that is experienced by him. When the mind is agitated, sorrow is experienced and when it is tranquil, there is joy. **Happiness, therefore, is measured by the tranquillity of one's mind.**

Man, the roof and crown of creation, has the unique capacity of quietening his mind without helplessly depending upon the objects around him. But this capacity now lies dormant in him and he, unaware of it, foolishly tries to procure happiness through the objects of the world, which have only a false glitter of joy. They can give, indeed, no enduring and everlasting satisfaction.

Our great religious books help us to awaken and promote this dormant faculty in man. He need not run after the sense objects to attain some fleeting experience of joy. He can get engaged in a more permanent and a fuller happiness, which is wholly independent of the availability of agreeable objects and environment. Such a man stands like a beacon light emitting the light of perfection, which serves as a guide to those who are still being tossed about in the sea of life's turbulence.

5. THE DUAL PATH

Material prosperity, by itself, cannot provide happiness to an individual, if he has not developed a healthy inner personality with a keen aptitude for living life dynamically and fully. Intelligent self-restraint and discipline, as prescribed in our scriptures, create such an aptitude.

Self-control and discipline are detested by the modern man who considers them as shackles put on his natural freedom and, therefore, he repels any idea of spiritual practice. This feeling is naturally aroused in those who are not trained to follow religious injunctions and precepts with an opportunity to intelligently understand and appreciate their efficacy as a practical code of healthy living. Unintelligent denial of sense enjoyment causes mental suppression, which leads to frustration or cynicism. This is responsible for the general abhorrence for religion.

To condemn religious precepts on the above score is like calling a dog mad and killing it; for religion helps man's personality to blossom forth, enjoy a better and more cheerful life. An intelligent and proper understanding of the laws governing man's inner personality inspires higher ideals and gives him a broader vision of life. As man progresses in his inward expansion, the lower tendencies in him automatically drop off. The consequent rejection of lower values following his higher understanding is sublimation (as opposed to suppression), which the scriptures envisage. Notwithstanding one's knowledge of good and bad, and the guidance provided by religious doctrines, one seems to constantly gravitate to the lower and vulgar actions of life. It is so amazing that man knowingly chooses a path, which is detrimental to his ultimate prosperity. The great Ṛṣis investigated into this question and arrived at clear and precise conclusions.

There are two distinct and separate paths in life, namely, **the path of the pleasant** (preya) and **the path of the good** (śreya). Man is confronted with the choice of taking to one of these paths at every single moment of his life. The path of pleasant, as the name suggests, pleases, fascinates and entices man to take to it. Whereas, the path of the good, which is based on sound religious precepts and injunctions, is resisted by the human mind.

The path of pleasant which caters to man's self-gratification provides immediate pleasures, but ultimately, putrefies into enlarging ripples of disappointment and sorrow.

In striking contrast, **the path of good is detested in the beginning but, later on; it leads to greater happiness and a sense of fulfilment.**

Religion can be likened to a kindly policeman directing mankind to the path of the good, but the irresolute mind tries to gain immediate flickers of joy, by choosing the other. Man is thus, denied an opportunity of having a greater and serener happiness, which the scriptures provide. All men of determination and discrimination choose the right path and lead the rest of humanity to lasting peace and happiness.

6. HARMONY OF EXISTENCE

Life is defined as a series of continuous experiences. An experience, therefore, becomes a unit of life just as a brick, is the unit of a wall. The strength or weakness of a wall depends upon the quality and texture of the bricks used in its construction. Similarly, experiences, being the units of life, will determine the type of life led by an individual. If his experiences are happy, his life is happy and if they are miserable, he is miserable.

The solution to the problems of life, therefore, lies in streamlining our experiences. The religious masters in this country after arriving at this conclusion, analysed thoroughly the structure of an experience and observed that every experience is constituted of three essential factors, viz., the experience; the object experienced and the relationship binding the two together, called the experiencing. The field of enquiry of these subjective scientists, was confined to the realm of the experiencer, who comes in contact with the multiple objects of the world, and gains his experience.

Pursuing the analysis further, and after scientific experimentation, they discovered, that the experiencer is a composite structure of four different personalities, viz., the physical, the emotional, the intellectual and the spiritual. They are so subtle and, at the time of experiencing, they all work so simultaneously and so quickly that the superficial observer fails to recognize their fine distinctions in a single action.

When the subject, experiencer, comes in contact with an object, he does so with four distinct instruments of experience operating from the four layers of his personality within. Each one of the four entities is differently constituted and has its own values and demands. In every situation created by an object, all the four rise up yearning to experience it.

Consider, for example, a sweet offered disrespectfully to an individual. The physical man in him rushes out to eat it and even his mouth starts watering. Notwithstanding the physical craving for tasting the sweet, the emotional personality in him resists it because of the manner in which it was offered. Again, the intellectual factor in him independently evaluates the situation and decides that, being a diabetic patient, sweet is detrimental to his health. Lastly, his spiritual personality forbids him to eat irregularly but urges him to develop self-control and avoid excessive and unintelligent indulgence in sense enjoyment.

The fourfold personality layers are like the antennae of an insect, which collect the experience from environmental objects and situations. When these aspects in an individual, each entertaining independent values of life, come in contact with an object or situation, the union may result in satisfaction for one or two of the layers, but produce a sense of dissatisfaction for the other layers. Consequently, a friction is generated in his personality and such friction, arising from a series of experiences, causes the individual to suffer the stress and strain of life, which is a common malady in the world today.

In this scheme of experience, and the confusion of personalities within, man's attempt at peace and tranquillity, his hope to live in smile and cheers, and his ambition to gain bliss, is shattered and he is driven to a chasm of despair, despondency and dejection, popularly called saṁsāra.

The stalwarts in the religious field discovered the methods by which man can properly integrate the four entities in him into one synthetic whole, and thereby, enjoy a harmony and rhythm in the varied experiences of life. The religious books, thus, provide practical suggestions and exercises, which, when followed sincerely and faithfully at all the four levels of personality create in one, the desired integration. The greater the integration in man, the greater is his freedom from the thraldom of the challenges in life.

The scriptures, no doubt, show us the path to a healthier and more intelligent living, but our determination and concerted efforts alone, can help us to achieve it.

7. PERSONALITY REHABILITATION

In every experience in life, man contacts the world through the media of four constituent entities in him. They are his body, mind, intellect and the Consciousness, which is the life spark in him. Of these, the mind and intellect equipment is the actual experience, that enjoys or suffers the object with which it comes in contact. When this equipment is perfectly tuned up, man experiences a harmony and rhythm in life, but when it lies neglected and fallen into disuse, there arises discord and harshness.

The physical body is the grossest aspect of the human personality, which contains the five organs of perception and the five organs of action. The size and shape of the body differ from individual to individual, but the essential material composing it, and the functions of the organs are common to all. Again, the subtlest aspect, namely, the Consciousness, which is the core of man's composite personality, is one and the same in all human beings.

The religious thinkers, after having scientifically discovered that these two aspects are common to mankind, proved by logical analysis and deduction that the variable factor in man is the mind and intellect equipment. The kaleidoscopic pattern of experience is, therefore, attributed to the difference in the texture and quality of the mind and intellect.

The mind is the seat of all emotions and feelings whereas the intellect is the discriminating faculty, the discerning factor, the judging ability, whereby man distinguishes the good from the bad, the right from the wrong and the real from the unreal. The functions of the mind and intellect are fundamentally divergent and opposed to each other. For example, when a person is overwhelmed with emotions, his faculty of discrimination is lost and when acute discrimination prevails, there is no room for his sentiments and feelings.

It is the subtle equipment, which is utilized by us in our day-to-day experiences in life. In fact, when one meets and deals with another, it is only the mind and intellect of one, which comes in contact with the mind and intellect of the other. When the quality and texture of the mind and intellect undergo any change in either of them, they are no longer interested in meeting each other. The actual 'Experiencer' in us, therefore, is the indwelling mind and intellect, and the body serves only as a garb worn by it. Consider, for instance, an individual visiting a friend's house. He does so only to contact the resident in the house and his interest in the visit is lost when the latter is not there. Similarly, our physical bodies are mere hutments in which the subtler personality dwells and all our contacts and experiences are transacted in the subtler realm.

In the world today, this important aspect of the human personality lies neglected and putrefied. It is no fault of man, since he knows not the state of his inner personality. Religion holds a mirror up to man's real nature within and also provides him with the 'ways and means for chastening his emotions' and 'edifying his thoughts', thereby enabling him to live a more dynamic and cheerful life.

The mind and intellect of man, like the yolk and the white of an egg, need to be carefully tended and nurtured in the warmth of Mother Śruti (scriptures) in order that they may develop and usher him into a freer and ampler existence. But, when they are neglected, his personality degenerates and creates disturbances and chaos for himself and the society. It is, therefore, necessary for us to put forth our efforts in the direction indicated by the scriptures to enable us to grow inwardly, and help in bringing about a progressive and healthy society.

8. MIND AND MAN

The human personality is determined and defined by the quality and texture of one's mind and intellect. Religion helps to bring about a revolution in the individual's personality by chastening the mind and educating the intellect. By bringing about this change, man improves the state of his mind and develops subtler discrimination, thereby enabling him to enjoy a happier and more harmonious relationship with the ever-changing phenomenon of the external world of beings and happenings.

Since man's personality derives its essence from the structure of his mind and intellect, all schemes and plans envisaged by religion for personality rehabilitation are meant to promote development and perfection of this subtle equipment in him. Before attempting to rehabilitate us, therefore, it becomes primarily necessary for us to study and understand the nature, location and functions of the inner equipment in the human system.

The mind is the seat of im pulses and feelings and it is common to all living creatures. Animals also possess a mind. When they come in contact with the world, impulses or feelings are generated in their minds and these are straight away manifested in their respective actions. Thus, when you pull a dog by its tail, it gets a feeling of anger, which it expresses by barking at you. The dog does not have the capacity to judge and determine the intention and motive behind your action. It acts merely on the impulse received by its mind.

Man alone, being the roof and crown of creation, has the capacity to discriminate and analyse his feelings, as and when they arise and allow his actions to be guided and directed by his power of discrimination, instead of being driven and carried away by momentary impulses and feelings. This faculty of discrimination, the power of judgment, this capacity to discern what is right and what is wrong, what is to be done and what is not to be done, is the function of the intellect. The dignity and culture of mankind lie in the exercise of this faculty and when this wondrous equipment is left neglected, man is bound to deteriorate to the status of an animal and suffer the consequences thereof.

In our day-to-day experiences in the civilized and modern society, most of our actions seem to emanate from the realm of the mind and we are misled by feelings instead of being guided by discrimination. We do a thing simply because we 'feel like' doing it.

The intellect is generally divorced from the mind; There is, therefore no discrimination and considered choice in the actions. Such actions, depending upon the whims and fancies of our feelings, are detrimental and dangerous to our welfare and prosperity. Religion helps us to keep the intellect alert and apply its faculty of discrimination to the choice of right action at every moment of our life. Being guided by proper discrimination, such actions are dynamic and productive, and they bring about peace and cheer in society.

The mind, is like the receiving clerk in an office. Though the clerk receives the mail, he does not take action on them, but puts them up to the officer in-charge for his direction and advice for disposal. But if the clerk chooses to take action directly, without consulting the officer, there is bound to be confusion and chaos in that organization. This in short, is the sad state of affairs about the human system of the modern age. Our minds receive impulses from the external world, and we respond directly without the guidance or control of the intellect, which is the officer in-charge within our body politic. Consequently, there is confusion and chaos within, leading naturally to dissatisfaction and discontentment in life.

The mind is defined as a 'flow of thoughts' just as a river is a flow of water. The banks of the river guide and direct its flow and when the banks are not firm, the water runs amok. So too, when the intellect of man is not firm and determined, the mind functions as it wants, and man is tossed hither and thither by the vicissitudes of his environment and circumstances. To keep the intellect firm and determined and to be constantly guided by the dictates of such an intellect is the training imparted by religion.

The **secret of success** behind all **men of achievement** lies in the faculty of applying their intellect in all their activities without being misled by any surging emotions or feelings. Religion offers the **technique of development** of this faculty and leaves the choice to man to make or mar himself and his progress.

9. THE PATH OF PERFECTION

The mind and intellect is the essence of the human personality. The physical body, to repeat, is merely a garb worn by it. The quality and texture of mind and intellect equipment in us depend upon our inherent and innate tendencies or inclinations, which are called vāsanās. Philosophy and religion serve as architects in moulding and reshaping man's vāsanās and thereby rehabilitating and adjusting his personality.

The five sense organs are windows in the human structure through which the stimuli from the external world of objects reach us. The eyes take in the forms and colours; the ear receives the sounds; the nose, the smell; and so on. The mind and intellect reacts to these stimuli and responds to them in the form of actions, which are executed by the five organs of action in the physical body. The continuous transaction of the receipt of stimuli and the corresponding responses echoing out of the human system, constitute the 'traffic of life'. Where and when this transaction has ended, life becomes extinct.

Religion is like a friendly policeman who guides man through this 'traffic of life' to reach the goal of a perfectly happy and successful life. The external world of objects is in a constant flux of change, depending upon the vicissitudes of nature. All living creatures are affected and victimized by these changes occurring in the environments and circumstances. But man alone has the unique capacity to neutralize adverse stimuli reaching him and produce out of them responses, which bring about harmony and melody in existence. This consummation is achieved by the wondrous equipment of the mind and intellect. In order that we may maintain a healthy relationship with the world and not fall under the suzerainty of the exigencies of life, the maintenance of healthy and powerful mind and intellect is of utmost importance. This means that our emotions must be chaste and our intellectual discrimination subtle and clear.

In our experience in life, we find that we are, what we are, because of the calibre of the mind and intellct equipment in us. If we are full of feelings of love, tenderness and kindness, we are naturally loving and kind and if the power of our discrimination is sharp and brilliant, we are bound to be brilliant. The environment and circumstances may be disagreeable and disturbing but, as long as our inner equipment is healthy and strong, none of them can influence or disturb our peace, stability and tranquility. Such a man stands erect and motionless like a towering lighthouse, unaffected by the surging waves, which strike against it and die away. But when this subtle equipment is neglected or kept in disuse, the individual is like a 'neglected boat' in the ocean of life, tossed hither and thither by the calamitous waves of challenges.

The structure and composition of the individual mind and intellect are founded upon his own vāsanās, which primarily determine the type of reactions and responses emanating from his person. Thus, when our vāsanās or tendencies are dynamic, our thoughts and actions are dynamic and productive, but when they are dull and inert, our thoughts and actions are lifeless and unproductive. The entire personality and reconstruction, which provides the solution to man's progress, peace and prosperity, therefore, rests on the development of proper innate tendencies. Religion provides for such development by holding a mirror up to our nature and educating us on the realities of things. Thus, by purifying and reforming the vāsanās, the mind and intellect get properly tuned up and perfected and with such equipment, one is well armed to face any challenge in the world and to emerge victorious and ride over it.

A nation is built by the individuals comprising it. When each individual in the society or nation puts forth his effort in the direction indicated in the scriptures and reconstitutes his personality, then, that society or nation grows dynamically, permeating peace and glory to one and all. **Let us therefore, awake, arise and rebuild our nation and ourselves.**

10. THE MECHANISM OF ACTION

In the mechanism of human action, the propelling force behind our desires, thoughts and actions originates from our innate inclinations and tendencies, called by the term 'vāsanās'. Though our activities appear to be defined by our tendencies, man has the unique capacity, which is denied to all other living creatures, to exercise this self-effort in choosing his actions. By a persistent and prolonged application of this great faculty, every human being can erase his inherent tendencies and reach the pinnacle of perfection.

An analysis of the genesis of our action provides an interesting study of the human system. Every action perpetrated, is the fulfilment and culmination of a desire in an individual, while his desire is the gross manifestation of the subtle tendencies in him. Thus, when the nature of his tendencies is to speculate and gamble, he entertains a desire to do so. The desire in the medium of such tendencies soon crystallizes in the form of a thought. The thought helplessly draws him to gambling houses or such other fields where his particular desire could be entertained. Man's tendencies or vāsanās are the prime mover of all his desires and action and, as long as they last, desires keep springing up in his bosom and create mental agitation and discontentment with life as such.

Vāsanās in saṁskṛt mean fragrance. Each individual has vāsanās, distinct and peculiar to him and they constitute and define his individuality. In other words, an individual is nothing but a substantial form of his vāsanās. The heterogeneous pattern of human beings is explained by the variety and differences in the texture of vāsanās composing them. However, when man gets rid of his vāsanās, he transcends mental agitation and attains a divine status. This idea is beautifully symbolized in the lighting of camphor before an idol. Camphor is nothing but fragrance consolidated, since a pure sample of it, on exposure, spontaneously sublimates and fills the atmosphere with its fragrance. Camphor is lit before a deity and, as it burns away, we get the vision of the Lord. So too, as our vāsanās are eradicated, the divinity within us is unfolded and we begin to experience our inner divine nature.

From the study of origin of action, it appears as though one is left with no choice but to act as per one's own tendencies. This is not true in the case of human beings. Animals are however, victimized by their tendencies and they have no option. For instance, a tiger has a tendency to strike and kill and consequently his desires, thoughts and actions are barrelled in that direction. He has little discretion to live apart from his ferocity and destructive nature.

Desires and thoughts spring forth from one's vāsanās just as sounds emanate from the etchings in a gramophone record. But man, the sovereign of all creations, possesses a singular capacity to stand apart from the surging desires and feelings and exercise his self-effort in choosing the right action. When this great faculty is consistently applied, in the direction indicated by the scriptures, he successfully eradicates his vāsanās and emerges out in his infinite nature.

Thus, looking back into our past, we are helpless victims of our past actions but looking ahead of us, we become the architects of our own future. Human as we are, let us never look back for a moment but dynamically march forward creating a glorious future of magnificent achievements by rightly exercising the independent self-effort, which is man's prerogative.

11. THE LAW OF KARMA

Man's diverse tendencies or vāsanās are the prime movers of all his desires and actions. As long as vāsanās exist, desires continuously spring forth in his bosom and create mental agitation and discomfort, resulting in actions. These actions in turn, leave imprints in our personality as vāsanās, which influence and propel our future actions. This cycle is based on a law called 'Law of Karma', which is one of the significant contributions of the philosophy of Vedānta to humanity.

It is a law based on pure scientific reasoning covering the past, the present and the future and it is as much applicable to mankind and life as any other law of nature. Many hasty readers have misunderstood the law of karma as a mere law of destiny and condemned it as a pessimistic and ineffectual theory dealing only with one's past experiences in life. The following analysis of it should clear the cobwebs of misunderstanding and reveal its original beauty and strength.

Man is, what he is because of his past actions. If his experiences from the time of his birth to the present moment are pure and noble, he is today a man of chastity and dignity; if on the contrary, they are vicious and immoral, he takes to those qualities. In short, he is a product or an effect of his own past actions or karma. This is the principle of destiny. It may be concluded from this that man is a mere victim of his past actions over which he has no control. It then becomes an inert philosophy concerning the dead past which is incompatible with the modern scientific and progressive mind.

On the other hand, the law of karma is a vital force in the Vedānta philosophy, which enables man to be spirited and dynamic and to reach the goal of human existence. Destiny or 'prārabdha' is the product or the effect of the past and it forms one aspect of the law of karma. Man, is in a way, influenced by his destiny since his present status is caused by past. But, at the same time, he is gifted with the capacity to choose his present action, which is called self-effort or 'puruśārtha'. All along his life, he has been exercising this power gifted to him and an aggregate of all these past self-efforts has determined his present destiny. In other words, the sum total of all past puruśārtha will be equal to his present prārabdha. **'What' one meets in life is destiny and 'how' one meets it, is self-effort.**

The law of karma goes a step ahead of the law of destiny and states that the future lies in the control of man since he has the capacity to change it by regulating his self-efforts from now on. Thus, if he had chosen the path of the pleasant (preyas) in the past, no doubt he has to suffer the consequences of it at this moment, but his self-effort today may be exercised in choosing the path of good (śreyas) which combines with the past and makes his future better than his present. **The future, therefore, is a continuity of the past modified in the present.** The freedom to modify the past and to create a future, either for the better or for the worse, is puruśārtha or self-effort.

Though man enjoys freedom to choose his action, the effect of his actions is influenced by the past. In other words, his self-effort, when exercised, mixes with his destiny to bring about an effect, resultant of their combination. The idea is better understood with the following example; the rate of flow of water in a river is two miles an hour. A log of wood floating on the water will also move at the same speed as the water in the river. If now the log is fitted with a motor with an independent speed of 10 miles per hour, its speed will, in effect, be conditioned by the flow of the river. Its independent speed is no doubt 10 miles an hour, but when it is directed downstream it registers 12 miles an hour and when diverted upstream, the speed is reduced to 8. Similarly, man possesses the faculty of independent movement, which is found lacking in the animal and plant kingdoms. Its effect in life however, is modified by the play of his destiny upon it.

Looking back at the past, man is the product of it but looking into the future, man is a producer. At the present moment, he is a product-cum-producer, i.e. he is the son of his father and a father of his son as well, at one and the same time. The law of destiny only refers to his past and makes him a victim of it, while the law of karma infuses the spirit of creation by focusing his attention on the future. It explains at the same time, the limitations of self-effort, lest he should get discouraged by the effects produced. Thus the law of karma is governed by the scientific theory of cause and effect. Extending the law further, the Ṛṣis declared that it would be unscientific and illogical to confine the theory to the present life only. The effects experienced in the present life must have had their causes in the past lives and the causes created in the present shall grow into effects in the future.

The law of karma applies not only to an individual but to a community, society or a nation as well. Again, its application is not restricted to the present lives, but embraces those of the past and the future. This law enables one to view life in its entirety, which provides a meaning, a purpose and a rhythm to existence. To understand life without applying the law of karma is like seeing a life-size picture with eyes fixed at a distance of a few inches from the canvas; the totality of vision is lost and one develops a narrow constricted view of life.

The law of karma is an important limb of religion. Religion, therefore, is not a mere mechanical worship, but a scientific **formula for right living**. By adhering to it, man develops himself and enjoys a better and more purposeful life.

12. THE PLAY OF MIND

Religion is not a bundle of superstitions to be fumigated at regular intervals with incense and candlesticks. When carefully analysed, it is a definite **science of life** giving a complete **technique of practical living**. By faithfully adhering to its precepts and following its practical suggestions, man can make this world a better and happier place to live in.

Life is a series of experiences. The experiencer comes in contact with the world of objects and ekes out for himself pleasure or pain, joy or sorrow, success or failure. His reactions are dependent upon the quality and texture of his mind and intellect equipment. There is an infinite variety in the texture and composition of the equipment varying, as they do, from individual to individual. Each individual looks at the world in and through the medium of his own inner equipment, and gains the particular vision envisaged by it. Thus, the same world provides different and distinct visions as the equipment of the individual projects them.

Analysing a few examples, we find that to the scientist, the world appears to be a field of magnificent phenomena of the discovered and the undiscovered, of great power and potentialities; to a peasant in a remote village, the same world is insignificant with nothing spectacular about it. Again, to a poet, the world is a manifestation of nature in luxurious and extravagant beauty and he sees in it everywhere an expression of divinity. The wealth of beauty fills his heart with ecstatic joy, and yet we do not see what he sees and experiences. The same world is viewed by a pessimist as an inferno of misfortunes and tragedies. To him, everything in the world is repugnant and distressing. Hence, the objects remaining the same, the experiences differ from man to man, and the reaction gained by them depends upon the constitution of their inner equipment.

The world, therefore, has no precise and clear-cut definition. The pattern changes like a kaleidoscope according to individual vision. As for instance, a man wearing blue glasses sees the world blue and on changing them to green, he sees the world green. Realizing this truth, the religious masters advised man to reform and reconstruct his inner instruments of experience so that the world is interpreted by him in its true perspective. **'Master the mind and you master the world'** was their slogan.

Nevertheless man, in his innocence, still believes in the development and beautification of the external world more than the rehabilitation of his inner personality; consequently, there have arisen three types of workers who have sincerely served mankind, making this world a better place to live in. They are the economist, the politicians and the scientists.

The economist provided more wealth and material prosperity for the people. The politicians dealt with the people and improved the pattern of mutual and cooperative living. The scientists harnessed and tamed nature for man to enjoy it. These are undoubtedly great services; but man, seated amidst this luxurious world, projects his own world of sufferings and sorrows. It is like a rich and sumptuous dinner laid before a patient suffering from indigestion and nausea; the same food, which he would have normally eaten with gluttonous delight, appears repellent and painful even at sight.

True religion helps us to understand the world and ourselves. The world is nothing but a concrete objective projection of one's subjective feelings and thoughts. The development of the inner personality is the path indicated in all scriptures. Religion prescribes certain eternal values of life for man to practice and live up to. These values are common to all and are the laws of nature governing man and his relationship with the world.

The most fundamental of these eternal values are the three disciplines, namely brahmacarya (self-control); ahiṁsā (non-injury) and satyam (truthfulness), which are prescribed for regulation of our physical, mental and intellectual personalities respectively.

13. FUNDAMENTALS OF LIVING

There is nothing wrong with our times. It is a wonderful era of glorious achievements. And yet man, sitting in the midst of plenty and prosperity is undergoing stress and strain and can find no peace or happiness in life. The religious masters studied this sad paradox and discovered that man's mental make-up was the cause of all trouble. They also provided a remedy by prescribing certain fundamental values and virtues of life. These, when practised and lived, enable man to master his mind, and mastery of the mind is mastery over the world.

These values and rules of conduct are essentially the same in all religions, though there are some apparent differences attributable to the differences in the types of people to whom they were addressed and also the time and occasion when they were given out. However, the origin and source of them all are the three fundamental moral and ethical codes of behaviour, and they are brahmacarya (self-control); ahimsā (non-injury) and satyam (truthfulness). The disciplines advised here refer to the three layers of our personality viz., the physical, the mental or emotional and the intellectual, respectively.

The physical entity in man longs for contact with the world of objects for gaining sense gratification. The eyes wish to see beautiful forms and colours, the tongue craves for good food, the nose likes to smell pleasant fragrance and so on. Thus when an individual continues to live on mere gratification of his sensual demands, his passions breed and swarm in legions, which ultimately mutilate and consume him. To avoid such self-afflicted ills, brahmacarya was prescribed as a disciplining at the physical level.

Brahmacarya means living in self-control with respect to all our sense enjoyments and does not mean their total denial. The world of objects is meant for us to enjoy and the scriptures do not deny us the freedom to enjoy them. They merely advise us to be masters of our enjoyments, and not allow them to dominate and enslave us. With a heart full of love, our preceptors cry out, **"Enjoy the world, but let not the world enjoy you. You may eat food, let not the food eat you. You may drink but let not the drink, drink you".**

The interpretation of the word 'brahmacarya' has been so badly contorted and distorted that the real significance and value of this discipline has been lost. It is popularly misunderstood to mean complete abstinence from sexual life. This is absurd. What the Mahātmās advice us is to abstain from excessive indulgence in any sensual pleasure. In short, to talk too much or to listen to a radio all day would be breaking the vow of brahmacarya. If this sacred doctrine is not followed, man abdicates his own freedom and becomes a slave to the ever-changing environment and circumstances.

The second discipline, prescribed for the mental level, is ahiṁsā, which means non-injury. Ahiṁsā does not mean non-killing or non-injury at the physical level. Sometimes we may have to be cruel and injurious externally even though our heart behind our actions is full of love and kindness. It is therefore, to be understood as a mental attitude to our relationship with others in life. Shakespeare has beautifully expressed this idea in his Hamlet, "I am cruel only to be kind". For example, a surgeon may appear cruel and bloody while performing his operations, but his heart means well. Such actions, though physically hurting and causing pain, would still fall under ahiṁsā.

The third principle is 'satyam' or truthfulness, a value of life on the intellectual plane. Satyam enjoins that one should live honestly with one's own intellectual convictions. Every one of us has ideals of his own, but only a few live up to them. We are led to compromise with our ideals when temptations induce us and we fall prey to our senses. This is asatyam or dishonest living. **The dignity of man lies in living up to his own convictions at all times.**

The edifice of life stands on these great principles. We shall follow them and let humanity rise to eminence and glory.

14. HARMONY AND POISE

In the world today, we are living through an age of confusions and tensions both within and without. The external challenges persecute us and render our lives unhappy and sorrow-ridden. The intelligent philosophy of the Ṛṣis advises man **to live in harmony with the situations in life and steadily work on to meet them with discretion and constant application.** When we live thus for a period of time, a subjective poise develops, giving us inward peace and tranquillity which thereafter, remains unaffected by external threats and onslaughts.

In the outer world of bitter competition and immoral strife, each one of us is compelled to battle constantly with things and beings. Deep within ourselves also, we have become helpless slaves to our own uncontrollable desires and undisciplined thoughts. Thus, modern man comes to shreds and is torn asunder between the two forces; the objective tensions and the subjective confusions.

The external threats and challenges are bound to reach us time and again and none can escape them. Hence, the success and joy in one's life are measured by the extent of control one has over the inner subjective confusions. In our experience in life, we fall into detestable and distressing environment and circumstances, which provoke and enrage us, and we despair for a solution. Such heart-burning protests and indignation weaken our inner personality and this weakness lends strength and might to the external challenges. In short, instead of braving the challenges, we render ourselves impotent and become ineffective and allow the external challenges to crush and consume us.

After carefully analysing our weaknesses, the masters in the religious fields advise us to grow in strength and gain mastery over situations in life by living in harmony with them. **The life of harmony can be lived by rising above our limited egocentric view of things and happenings, and expanding our mind to accommodate a constant awareness of the totality of the world, the entirety of mankind and the vastness and wholeness of the universal problems.** When this total and consummate perception is developed and maintained, man's individual problems sink into insignificance and absurdity.

But, when man views his problems from a purely egocentric and individual angle without this vision of totality, problems assume exaggerated and enormous proportions and crush him. Such a man is like a musician in the orchestra who chooses to play on his own without falling in line with the general rhythm and melody of the entire chorus of the orchestra. Hence, to live a life of harmony, is to recognize oneself, at every moment, to be a member of the entire humanity living in a composite universe and merge one's life with the resonant cadence of the whole, and bring about a fascinating melody of harmonious existence.

The principle of living in harmony with the external world is not to be construed as a life of ideal acceptance or unintelligent surrender to the challenges confronting us. The apparent harmony detected by the humble and impotent adaptors to challenging situations is worse than the dullness of death, while the harmony envisaged by our religious masters is the dynamic silence, which is the architect of all creations. This art of practising harmony is to be applied in the din & roar of the market place while we are heaving and sweating with exertion upon the narrow path of uncertainties in life.

Our life of harmony with the ampler scheme of the cosmos brings to our heart an inward peace and poise. When poise is maintained within us, problems and challenges vanish like mist before the rising sun.

Religion helps us to live the life of harmony and gain poise in personality. Let us follow her precepts, gain self-mastery and lead humanity to success and eternal glory and peace.

15. SCIENCE AND RELIGION

The history of the evolution of human intellect passes through four distinct stages, culminating in perfection, which our religious masters attained. Philosophy and religion relate to the fourth and the final stage of intellectual development, which is far ahead of all scientific knowledge known to mankind. Not knowing this truth, man scoffed at and rejected religion as antiquated and behind the times; consequently the progress of human evolution was arrested, leading to stagnation and general decadence that the world suffers from today.

In the beginning of human development, man was led by instincts and impulses rather than reason and knowledge. He merely perceived the phenomenon of nature, the sun and the moon, the rain and the thunders, birth and death and so on. His perception was no better than that of animals, for, in both the cases their intellect never reacted to the external world. He enjoyed himself whenever objects and environment were pleasant and agreeable, but suffered silently when they were unpleasant and disagreeable. He never questioned or tried to improve what he perceived. This was the 'Age of Perception'.

From this crude and barbarous age of perception, humanity marched forward to reach the 'Age of Observation'. Man was no longer content with mere perception; he began to ponder over the why and the wherefore of the phenomenon of nature around and about him. His intellect thus started the causation hunting.

For example, the primitive generation living in the age of perception, took to shelter when the rains poured down and emerged when the rains ceased. They merely perceived and experienced the rainfall, but were never curious to observe it and much less interested in enquiring into its cause. But, as man advanced in his intellectual development, he became more observant and began to wonder at the phenomenal power of nature. His little intellect observed certain simultaneous occurrences and related them unintelligently to the rainfall. Thus, when he found a mango tree shaking whenever it rained, he attributed the cause of the rain to the shaking of the mango tree. This was the 'Age of Observation' or superstition where effects were traced to causes, which were beyond any scientific reason and logic.

As humanity evolved further, man advanced to the 'Age of scientific Enquiry', when his intellect reached a higher stage of development. He sought to discover the cause of everything around and about him. He penetrated into the working of the phenomenal world, collected data and facts, experimented upon them, drew intelligent and rational conclusions and laid down a systemized knowledge of laws. Superstitions and wild belief were substituted by scientific truths. No more did they believe that the shaking of the mango tree caused the rains.

The scientific age continues to discover the secret powers of nature for blessing society. The physicists and the chemists, the botanists and the mathematicians, the economists and the politicians, are all exercising their efforts and contributing to the endless discoveries of the laws of nature. This, in short, is the age in which we are living today. As the scientists are continuously pursuing their work in their respective fields of enquiry, a time comes when they, in their maturity, wonder at the harmony and rhythm expressed in the various laws of nature and start contemplating as to who is that eternal law-giver, who orders these laws to function in strict perfection, obedience and reverence. Thus, their objective enquiry is elevated to a subjective contemplation upon the primeval cause for everything that exists in nature and this marks man's entry into the 'Age of Contemplation'.

All the great religious masters were men of profound contemplation engaged in subjective research of the truth that binds all the laws of nature. The men of contemplation were not content with the mechanical discovery of the laws, but endeavoured to understand and discover, **the lawgiver, the controller and regulator of all laws.** It should, therefore, be quite clear from the foregoing that philosophy and religion are far ahead of science and its proud discoveries, and those who treat them as ancient and old-fashioned, have failed to understand their place and significance in the history of human development.

Let scientific discoveries go on and bless mankind. But those fortunate few who have evolved further to understand and appreciate the existence of a common denominator in the phenomena of nature, should progress further and discover the eternal law of all laws, the knowledge of all knowledge.

16. WHAT IS RELIGION?

True religion possesses two important limbs, namely, its philosophy and its ritualistic injunctions. Mere ritualism, bereft of philosophy, is only superstition, while bare philosophy without ritualistic practices is tantamount to madness. Both the aspects must go hand in hand. Philosophy reinforces the external practices of ritual and gives them a purpose and a goal for realization. Together, they bring out the meaning, significance and purpose of religion. Philosophy is the theoretical aspect of religion which, with scientific and rational analysis, elucidates the why and the wherefore of life and the universe, and contains a coherent system of thought for interpreting the reality. The ritualistic injunctions deal with the practical aspect of religion and lay down the spiritual practices to be followed for reaching the ultimate goal in life.

Religion, therefore, is a happy and intelligent blending of philosophy and ritualism. If the two aspects are not synchronized properly, there can be no religion. Unfortunately, however, man commits the blunder of projecting only one of these two aspects and calls it religion and attributes its decadence and failure to religion as such. True religion, in fact, knows no failure. Ritualism here, does not mean mere physical performance of ceremonies but also embraces all modes of practical religion, applicable to mental and intellectual levels of our personality. It, therefore, includes rites, ceremonies and duties practised externally, devotion or bhakti cultivated by the mind and subtle discrimination and meditation undertaken by the intellect. When man endeavours to translate the high philosophy, values and virtues of life to practical living, he encounters several difficulties, which has caused religion to sink into oblivion. These values are opposed to and come in conflict with man's extrovert nature. This constitutes one of the main obstacles.

An unintelligent and abrupt denial of sensual pleasures and a blind following of spiritual values results in suppression in an individual and this suppression for a period of time leads into bitterness, frustration and cynicism in life. If, however, one chooses the other alternative and continues indulgence in sensual pleasure, the senses being so strong and overpowering, pull him down into the abyss of carnality and animalism and any attempt, thereafter, to live a spiritual life will be next to impossible.

The religious masters arrived at a solution of the problem by prescribing an intelligent formula by which man could sublimate to a higher spiritual living. They held that physical indulgence might be well regulated but not denied to the extent of causing suppressions and frustrations. There must be a basic and initial self-control based on an intelligent appreciation of the philosophy underlying it. To the extent an individual regulates his sense indulgence; to that extent he must acquire the intellectual education of the higher values of life and consequent understanding of the futility of such indulgence. Conversely, to the extent he apprehends and digests the higher and nobler ideas governing life, he can afford to live self-restraint. Thus, by a mutual intelligent adjustment of study and application, man can sublimate and reach the peak of perfection and bliss.

It, therefore, becomes imperative for us to carefully regulate the doses of philosophical study and ritualistic practice. Mere performance of rituals without understanding their meaning and significance is superstitious living which, when prolonged, distorts our personality. On the other hand, learning the entire philosophy and keeping the knowledge to ourselves is to be like a donkey carrying gold on its back. Hence, let us take the valuable advice of our Ṛṣis and try to be religious in the true sense of the term.

17. VITALS OF A NATION

A population living in a geographical area would not by itself constitute a nation. It is just a mere number, a multitude of human beings. But, **when the members live together with an integrated programme and strive with diligence and devotion for the achievement of a common goal, one sees the formation and glorious achievements of a nation.**

As long as human beings live disintegrated, each one self-centred and seeking his private ends, regardless of others, with no allegiance whatsoever to a common cause, they can never make a nation. The scientific, economic and political philosophies have, time and again, given out revolutionary schemes, which present an artificial look of integration during the initial enthusiasm, but, by themselves, none of these schemes can ever succeed in creating or building up a true nation.

The schemes of the objective scientists never deal with man as such. They are only concerned with the environments and circumstances and not with the individual. But a nation is composed of individuals, and its nature and strength are essentially rooted in the texture and quality of the individuals comprising it. How then could a nation be built by mere enhancement of wealth, improvement of social laws or advancement of science and technology?

This does not mean that the political revolution, economic planning and scientific progress are to be disregarded or cast aside. Wealth, amenities and social orders have, no doubt, their own particular significance, but they go only as far as they can, and will be rendered negative if the individuals manning them are wanting in integrity of character, which constitutes the very backbone of a country.

The political workers introduce dogmas, bring about reforms and endeavour to ensure that their country looks the best in the eyes of the world. Nevertheless, when the individuals in any country have no national consciousness or a feeling of love and fraternity, internal struggles and strifes arise and sap the very root of the politician's idea of a united and progressive nation. Many a great empire has thus met its downfall and sunk into oblivion.

Again, in the economic field, the economists try to bring about wealth and material prosperity to the nation, but, material prosperity, whatever be its dimensions, can achieve no purpose worth the name without integrity and strength of character amongst the people at large. Where there is moral and cultural degradation, there is bound to be aggrandizement and exploitation, culminating in impoverishment.

Similarly, **all scientific achievements can be a blessing to mankind only as long as man is rational and ethical.** But, if he loses his discrimination and flouts all moral and ethical values of life, employs his knowledge in destructive channels, these achievements become a curse and threat to mankind. This is what we find in the human situations of the day. Whatever be the development and progress in the objective fields of enquiry, a population does not acquire the recognition or status of a nation, unless it is knit together with bonds of character and principles of service and sacrifice. This dynamic spirit of togetherness can be achieved by religion alone.

Philosophy is a 'Pure science of life and when translated into practical living, it is termed religion. In other words, religion may be said to be an 'Applied science of life'. A faithful adherence to religious precepts and doctrines develops a proper sense of integrity amongst individuals who go to constitute a healthy community. The coordinated and inspired efforts of such human beings alone can build up a nation.

A united country, wherein each citizen is inspired to give out his very best in a spirit of selfless dedication, demanding nothing for himself except the privilege of serving the country, develops into a mighty nation asserting itself with power, prestige and strength.

The dynamics of togetherness is, therefore, to be discovered immediately – more so, in the context of the present world. The answer to this great challenge of the times assures us of a continued future as a happy, united and progressive nation serving as a beacon for the restless world to follow and gain a more rewarding peace and a more meaningful progress.

18. WHAT IS CULTURE?

Culture is the measuring rod of civilisation. The difference between an uncivilised barbarous country and a civilised nation lies in their culture. When a set of people live for a long period of time in a particular geographical area, respecting certain philosophical values and virtues of life, there emanates a fragrance, which is called their culture. The quality of such culture depends upon the type of values followed. The first three aspects are common to different countries and they are the same within limits just as the head, the trunk and the limbs are common to all human beings although the size, weight, colour and shape differ from one another. **The difference in culture, therefore, lies in the values and virtues of life entertained by the people.**

The values reported by the people are, in the beginning, ordered by external exigencies of life. Thus, in the first age of civilisation, geographical and climatic conditions and environment influenced the people and determined their values of life. Once such values are determined and a culture is set, the external environment will have little influence over the culture thus established. In western countries, the land was rugged and hard because of severe climatic conditions and constant snowfall; consequently the people became hardy. They had to train themselves to fight unrelenting Nature and procure from her whatever was required for their self-preservation. Conquest of nature thus became a fundamental trait in the character of people in the West. In sharp contrast, the East provided land with plenty and prosperity. With the slightest persuasion, the land yielded an abundance of flowers, fruits and vegetation; rivers were ever full and springtime flourished for nearly eight to nine months in a year. In such harmonious expressions of life, everywhere the people imitated the nature and quite naturally developed a culture based upon 'serving and giving' instead of 'fighting and procuring'. Thus, a culture emanating peace, tranquillity and love, developed in this country, whereas materialism took roots in the West and inculcated the idea of conquest.

Even in our day-to-day experiences in life, we can clearly observe, how external environment and happenings exercise initially their distinct influence on the development of our culture. A poor boy, living in the rugged atmosphere of the slums, seems to develop a tendency to protest and fight, while another, born of opulence and security, is generally more refined and cultured. This can be observed even in a bus queue where the latter waits and takes his turn while the former often protests, rushes and forces himself in.

Civilization flourishes with the promotion of culture, but when cultural values deteriorate, the civilization of a society breaks down as we have seen in the fall of the Egyptian, Greek and Roman Empires. The great religious masters of this country, using their own ingenious efforts, have, time and again, revived the philosophical and religious values for which the country stood and thereby, arrested the deterioration of culture. When culture deteriorates, there is an increase in barbarism and immorality in the country and its philosophy is misinterpreted, leading to confusion and chaos among its people. This, in short, is more or less the sad condition of the present world. The need of the hour is to arrest this deterioration by reviving the great philosophical and religious values of life.

In no other literature in the world have these values been so beautifully and exhaustively dealt with as in the scared books of our country. Hence, **it becomes the bounden duty of each one of us, to dedicate oneself to unearthing the sacred messages of our scriptures and highlighting their philosophy, for the rest of mankind to follow and be blessed with.**

19. WHAT MAKES A MAN?

Man is the roof and crown of creation. Besides man, the manifested world comprises the animal, the plant and the inert kingdoms. After a scientific analysis of the categories of things and beings, the religious masters discovered a similar classification prevailing among human beings. Further, they declared on the basis of their own experiences that the noblest and the best among the human kingdom are within the reach of every man. Gradation among the human beings is created by the differences in the quality and texture of their emotions and intellectual convictions.

The inert objects merely exist, like the stone or the earth; they are neither conscious of, nor do they react to, the external world. We find a variety of human beings similar to insentient things. They are just as indifferent, as ignorant and as totally unaware of external circumstances and environment. The consciousness or awareness of the world in such people is vague and indistinct, and they are an embodiment of colossal lethargy and inertia, having no plans, no passions and no pangs in life. Such men may be classified as 'Stone-men'.

A little more evolved than the inert objects are the plants. Plants are also predominantly lethargic. They remain where they are and their reaction to the world is confined to basic necessities for their existence. The rudiments of discrimination seem to emerge in the plant kingdom. They are able to distinguish between sunlight and darkness, food and poison and they endeavour to obtain what they need. Emotions, however, are basically lacking in flora in as much as a mother tree does not allow even its seedlings to grow under it when the latter come in the way of its quest for food and water.

On a careful study and observation of mankind, we find among them a definite variety whose life imitates that of a plant. Such men, steeped in inertia, react only to exaggerated happenings. They can never exert or do anything constructive. They exercise discrimination only when the objects are gross and substantial and they lack the basic emotion or feeling for others. Such men fall under the category of 'Plant-men'.

Animals are more evolved and have a better awareness of the world. The faculty of intellectual discrimination has appreciably grown among animals as compared to that obtaining in the plant kingdom, and their reactions to the environment have naturally improved. They move from place to place in quest of food but do not perish like the plant if food is not available in their location. Emotions and feelings are found to have developed in the animals; they care, not only for themselves, but also for their offspring.

Similarly, among men, there are 'Animal-men' who are desire-ridden, passionate and egocentric. Their intellectual discrimination is limited and, being always extroverted, they constantly engage themselves in fighting, procuring and aggrandizing for the enjoyment of their kith and kin and themselves. In fact, a wide cross section of human beings belongs to this category and their activities are mainly guided by feelings and impulses rather than by discrimination and understanding.

The fourth variety is 'Man'– the best in creation. Human beings have the maximum capacity for emotion and their feelings can embrace the entire universe. Also, the faculty of intellectual discrimination in man knows no bounds; not only can he discriminate extrovertly in the realm of the gross world, but can also delve into the subjective layers of his personality until he reaches the recesses of the spiritual core in himself.

Those who do not make use of this great capacity inherent in them, belong to the aforesaid three categories, though they are labelled as 'Man'. But **the rare few that develop a universal love and constantly**

engage themselves in activity under the guidance of their superior intellect, are called 'Man-men' and they alone can claim the prestige, dignity and glory of man. Having taken the human embodiment, would it not be suicidal to lead a life in this world abandoning this wonderful faculty, bestowed on us by the kind Lord?

20. ESSENCE IN MAN

A man must know his real identity if he desires to maintain a proper and healthy relationship with the world at large. Every human being is constituted of physical, mental and intellectual equipment and the conscious principle, which lends sentience to this equipment. Human development culminates in finding one's identity with the conscious principle – the spiritual core of one's personality.

The physical body is the grossest aspect of our personality. The mind is the subtler equipment and the intellect, the subtlest of the three. The three together constitute matter, which by itself is inert and insentient. The Consciousness is the spirit in us, which propels, motivates and causes this equipment to function. The Consciousness without equipment has no experience or no activities of its own. It is the combination of the two viz. spirit and matter which causes the manifestation of life and activity.

A similar phenomenon, obtaining in the objective world, presents a clear idea of the structure and functioning of the human mechanism. The human equipment is like an electric bulb, a heater or a refrigerator. The bulb heater and the refrigerator have no capacity by themselves to light, to heat or to refrigerate until they come in contact with electricity, just as Consciousness functioning through the body-mind-intellect equipment manifests in life.

When man identifies with his physical personality, he merely lives as a physical personality, he merely lives as a physical being bereft of emotions and intellectual discrimination, and he constantly engages himself in fighting, procuring and aggrandizing wealth and the objects of the world for his sense gratification. Sensual desires are insatiable; the more they are sought for and indulged in, the more they swarm in legions. Thus man, living at the level of the body, is ever agitated and consumed by vain desires.

But, when man identifies himself with the emotional aspect in him, he lives on a plane higher than that of the former. His mind expands to accommodate the welfare of others as well. The feelings of love and brotherhood for others, provide him a better and subtler satisfaction than what mere physical indulgence can give. Consequently, his sensual demands surrender in favour of those whom he loves.

As man ascends higher and identifies himself with his intellect, he develops discrimination in the light of which his emotions and thirst for physical indulgence are dispelled. For example, a scientist or a politician, fired with an intellectual idea or ideology, has neither an emotional attachment to his kith and kin, nor a physical appetite to satisfy himself with, while he is engrossed in this work.

The core of the human personality is the Consciousness, which is the 'Life-centre' around which all the activities of the body, mind and the intellect revolve. It remains ever changeless and immovable like an axle in the wheel, but causes all changes and movements to occur. When man succeeds in identifying with this changeless, immovable conscious principle within him, he is no longer victimized by the changing phenomena of perceptions, emotions and thoughts, but becomes the supreme Lord of them all. The intellectual pursuits, emotional attachments and physical cravings of such a man naturally withers and falls away like petals of a flower when the fruit emerges.

Religion teaches us this art of focussing our attention on the spiritual core, which is our Real nature, and when we understand the infinite dimensions of our being, we develop, in our experience of the Supreme Bliss, a total dispassion for anything that the material world can offer.

21. THE PATH OF DIVINITY

Man is essentially divine. But the divinity in him is veiled by the unbroken series of desires and thoughts arising in his bosom. A variety of these grades and concentration of these create the variety of human beings. To remove the encrustation of desires and thoughts, and unfold the divinity inherent in man, is the ultimate goal envisaged by the scriptures.

A scientific analysis of the psychological being in man reveals three thought conditions under which the human mind functions. They are called in Vedānta, as the 'sattva', the pure and the noble; the 'rajas', the passionate and agitated, and the 'tamas', the dull and the inactive state. Combinations of these three states of mind, in various permutations, determine the individual personalities. In fact, the noble, ignoble or indifferent aspects in the character and conduct of persons are regulated by the proportion in which the three constituents are mixed.

Tamas is a state of the mind in complete inertia, indolence and heedlessness, where there is no consistency of purpose, softness of emotion or nobility of action. Rajas is a condition of mind when it is agitated and stormy, passionate and ambitious and constantly riddled with desires, emotions and activities. Sattva is the subtlest of the three – a state of mind with balanced joy, serenity and creative poise when human contemplation is available in its entire heritage.

These three types of thoughts form the material with which the human mind and intellect are composed. The difference between the mind and intellect is, therefore, only in their respective functions. The mind is an instrument of feelings and emotions while the intellect is the one, which discriminates and judges.

The human discrimination or discerning faculty falls under two distinct and different categories depending upon the field in which it operates. When discrimination is directed towards the world of objects, which is the realm of objective sciences, it is called 'gross intellect' (sthūla-buddhi). But the same faculty, when applied subjectively to discriminate between the spirit and the matter or the transcendental and the terrestrial, gains the status of 'subtle intellect' (sukṣma-buddhi).

This explains why a person, brilliant in his application in the material and the secular world fails to understand, much less appreciate, the subtler import of the scriptures. However sharp the gross intellect may be, it cannot penetrate and understand the Truth beyond the realms of matter. It is like attempting to use a sharp axe to shave one's beard.

Animals and even plants possess, to an extent, a rudimentary intellect to discriminate and understand the external world but they totally lack the subtle capacity to discriminate between the real and the unreal. Man alone has, in his subtle intellect, the unique capacity to delve into and beyond the layers of matter and recognize the divinity within. The divinity or the Self in us is obscured by the three different patterns of thoughts in our bosom. The thoughts flowing in our mind are manifestations of the related desire entertained by us. Hence, when the desires are overcome, the divinity within unfolds itself. The Bhagavad-gītā beautifully describes the three types of veiling over the Self caused by these desires.

The sāttvic or the pure and noble desires also veil the Self in us, but the veiling is like the smoke covering fire. Even a passing breeze removes the smoke; so too, a little prayer or meditation takes away the subtle desires. The rājasic desires are those that are passionate and egocentric and they cover the Self like dust on the mirror. In this case, an effort is necessary to wipe the dust off. Likewise, individual effort, as directed by religion alone, can remove these desires. The third type of desires, called the tāmasic, means those that are obstinate, arrogant and totally egoistic. The divinity lies enveloped in them like a foetus in a womb. The indication is that these desires cannot be removed forthwith by mere effort; it takes a good deal of a time and patience like that of a foetus to grow and emerge from the womb.

Religion helps us to chasten our desires and thoughts, so as to ultimately end them, and as we rise from the tamas to the rajas, divinity gradually unfolds itself and when, the last traces of the sāttvic desires are also eliminated, man becomes God.

22. THE STATE OF DIVINITY

Godhood is experienced in the state of thought extinction. It is a state of being, when the mind is totally transcended. **Divinity is the very nature and essence of man; but, it lies covered under the encrustation of thoughts.** When thoughts cease to erupt, man attains Godhood. Religion indicates the different paths to reality; it prescribes various techniques for the extinction of thoughts, by quietening and transcending the mind.

Mind is related to thoughts as river is related to water. A mind is not merely thoughts just as river is not merely water. It is the flow of water that makes a river. So too, it is flow of thoughts, which creates the mind. A mind, thus created, veils the divine Self within us. Scriptures aim at transcending the mind by arresting and ending the thought-flow and thereby unfolding the divinity inherent in us. The 'flow' in each case generates power and dynamism. A mere collection of water, however large it be, lies inert and powerless; when, however, it starts moving, it gathers strength and dynamism. So also, thoughts, flowing in rapid succession, create a dynamic mind which projects the apparently permanent, stable and concrete world experienced by us. A similar phenomenon is seen when the glowing point of a stick is swiftly revolved in darkness. The rapidity of its movement produces distinct and clear figures, which appear real. Another example of the same principle from the modern world is the movies. The pictures in a film are, by themselves, inert and insentient; but solid, substantial and sentient scenes appear on the screen when the film moves in the projector.

Human mind today, is completely out of control, flowing in all directions. It is like a river in spate. Our primary attempt should be to prevent the flow spreading in all directions by controlling, harnessing and regulating it. This is achieved by reinforcing the banks, which decide the direction of the flow. Hence, the intellect has to be chastened and chiselled with the help of Scriptures.

Again, the nature of the river is dependent upon the quality and texture of the water flowing in it. If the water is muddy, the river is muddy; if the water is fast, the river is fast and so on. Likewise, the thoughts are directly related to the mind, and the mind to man. As the thoughts, so the mind; as the mind, so the man. No man, therefore, can be changed or reformed unless his mind changes; and the mind can never change unless the structure and composition of the thoughts are changed.

A change in thoughts can be effected by three methods, namely, by reducing the quantity of thoughts, by improving the quality of thoughts and by giving a different direction to the thoughts. They are declared in Hinduism by the three wellknown yogas called the karma, bhakti and jñāna yogas respectively. In addition to these, a fourth yoga, called the hatha-yoga, is prescribed for those who are underdeveloped both in head and heart. By the practice of these yogas, the mind gets purified and is rendered fit for meditative flights. When such a mind is absorbed in meditation, the last traces of thoughts die away, leaving the meditator in a state of Absolute Bliss.

The four yogas prescribed in Hinduism cater to the entire cross section of humanity. No other religion in the world is as conspicuously endowed with such a catholicity of practical application. The world needs this knowledge as much as Indians do.

The state of divinity is not merely a personal achievement; it must culminate in a universal resurrection.

23. FUNDAMENTALS OF VEDĀNTA

Civilization of society increases with culture, and breaks down as cultural values deteriorate, as we have seen the fall of the Egyptian, Greek and Roman civilizations. Bhagavān Vyāsa arrested the deterioration in Indian culture by compiling the Vedas. The Buddha, in his time, revived it. Once again, in Bhagavān Śaṅkara's times, the culture of the country had deteriorated. When culture deteriorates, there is an increase in barbarism and immorality, philosophy is misinterpreted and utter disaster follows. Śaṅkara appeared at such a stage and brought about the great renaissance in Hinduism. Thus, many such mighty masters have contributed toward the maintenance of the great culture of this country.

Hinduism does not centre around any particular personality or book. In ancient India, men of wisdom spent their days in the lap of nature's beauty and luxuriance. The valleys and forests of the great Himālayas and the sacred Ganges were the teachers who kindled in their hearts a hunger to know the mysteries of the power that gives life to the lifeless. The reflections and revelations of these perfect masters formulated the scriptures, which later came to be known as the Vedas.

The Vedas are four in number, namely, Ṛg, Yajus, Sāma and Atharva. Each Veda is divided into three sections-these are called Mantra, Brāhmaṇa and Upaniṣad (Āraṇyaka). In the Mantra portion, we find the ecstatic admiration of nature's beauty, expressed in lyrical poetry by these contemplative seers. The Brāhmaṇa portion deals with rituals and sacrifices; they are meant for mental integration and self-purification. The last portion contains the philosophic wisdom known as Vedānta.

Besides the Vedas (Śruti), the scripture literature of this country includes the Smṛtīs, Itihāsas, and Purāṇas which contain philosophy, ethics, social sciences and laws of society and so on.

The Vedas were not written by any one individual – they are inspired declarations of several Ṛṣis from the height of their intuitive experience. And when they were absorbed in the **transcendental experience they had gone beyond the realm of 'I' and 'Mine'.** This explains why they never appended their names to the holy texts.

The material scientist enquired into the world of objects and, by close observation, intelligent and rational analysis, deduced scientific laws of nature. The Ṛṣis undertook with the same process of analysis and deduction, the subjective enquiry into the personality of man and gave out philosophy and religion. The difference between the two types of enquirers lay only in their respective fields of enquiry. Naturally, therefore, in the Upaniṣads, the discussion was about life and its meaning and purpose.

The term 'Life' is easier to understand by analysing and understanding its antonym, 'Death'. An organism is said to be dead when it completely ceases to receive or respond to the stimuli from external objects. In other words, 'Death' is a state of total cessation of experience. **Life, therefore, is defined as a continuous series of experiences**–anubhavadhāra.

Since life is a series of experiences, each experience becomes a 'unit of life' just as a brick is the unit of a wall. The strength or weakness of a wall will depend upon the quality and texture of the bricks constituting it. Similarly, the type of experiences that an individual goes through will determine the character of his life. If his experiences are happy, his life is happy and if they are miserable, his life is miserable.

An individual gains an experience when he receives and responds to a stimulus from the external world. An experience therefore is constituted of the following three entities: -

The Experiencer   – the subject

The Experienced – the object

The Experiencing – the relationship between the
                          subject and the object.

The field of enquiry of the Ṛṣis, was the
'experiencer', whereas that of the physical scientist was
the 'experienced'. **Investigation about the 'experiencer'
is philosophy, while investigation about the
'experienced' is science.**

The Ṛṣis tried to develop the inner personality
of man and make him independent of the environment
and happenings in his world. Thus, their goal was to
raise the **standard of life** in man.

The scientists, on the other hand, tried to beautify
and make the world a better place to live in; their
attempt was, therefore, directed to raising the **standard
of living**.

On a further analysis of an experience, we find
that our experiences emanate from different levels of
our personality. For example, when someone offers a
coffee disrespectfully to us, our physical personality
may want it, but our emotional and intellectual
personalities protest against it because of the attitude
with which it is offered. The Ṛṣis made a thorough
study and scientific analysis of the structure of a
human being and formulated his spirituo physical

personality. They discovered that human personality comprises the divine spark of life, called the Ātman, with five layers of matter enveloping it.

The Ātman, or the Self, is represented in the diagram by the sacred mystic symbol Om. The five concentric layers of matter enveloping the Ātman are called sheaths or kośas. The term 'sheath' indicates that it is a mere covering for something, which is more vital. Just as the sword and its sheath remain separate from each other, so too, there is no mutual contact between the divine spark of life and matter vestures covering it.

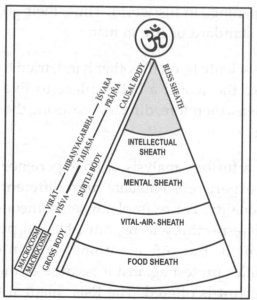

There are thus five distinct sheaths called Pañckośas (refer diagram).

1. The Food sheath or Annamaya kośa.
2. The Vital-air sheath or Prāṇamaya kośa.
3. The Mental sheath or Manomaya kośa.
4. The Intellectual sheath or Vijñānamaya kośa.
5. The Bliss sheath or Ānandamaya kośa.

1. The Food Sheath

The physical body, the outermost precincts of our personality, beyond which we do not physically exist is termed as the Food sheath. It is so called because it has emerged from the essence of food assimilated by the father and is nourished in the womb by the food taken by the mother; it continues to exist because of food eaten and it ultimately, after death, goes back to fertilize the earth and become food. The substance of the physical structure, rising from food, existing in food and going back to become food, is naturally and most appropriately termed as the Food sheath.

The Food sheath consists of the five sense organs or organs of perception, the jñāna-indriyas and five organs of action, karma-indriyas.

The five sense organs are the eyes, the ears, the nose, the tongue and the skin. The organs of action are speech, hands, feet, the genital organ and the organ of evacuation.

2. The Vital-air Sheath

The Pañca-prāṇas, which correspond to the five physiological systems described by the biologists, represent the Vital-air sheath. These activities which support the body take place as a result of the air that we breathe in. Hence it is termed as the Vital-air sheath. The five prāṇas of comprising this sheath are :-

(i) Prāṇas – The faculty of Perception : It controls the perception of the fivefold stimuli received from the outer world of objects through the five sense organs.

(ii) Apāna – The faculty of Excretion : All things thrown out of, or rejected by the body, such as seeds, sputum, perspiration, urine, faeces, etc. are expressions of 'apāna' .

(iii) Samāna – The faculty of Digestion : Digests the food received in the stomach.

(iv) Vyāna – The faculty of Circulation : The power by which the digested food is properly conveyed to the various limbs of the body by the blood stream.

(v) Udāna – The faculty of Thinking : The capacity in an individual to raise his thoughts from their present level so as to conceive a possibility of, or appreciate a new principle or idea, the capacity of self-education.

These five faculties gradually weaken as man advances in age. The Vital-air sheath controls and regulates the Food sheath. When the prāṇas do not function properly, the physical body is affected.

3. The Mental Sheath

The mind regulates and orders the Vital-air sheath. For example, when the mind is upset due to some shock, the functions of prāṇas and the body are affected.

A detailed study of the mind and intellect is as follows:

4. The Intellectual Sheath

The Intellect controls the mental sheath.

A comparative study of the Mind and Intellect:

To get a clear idea of what exactly the mind and intellect are, they have been differentiated below in five ways. This multiple differentiation serves to give us a clear and comprehensive picture of the exact significance of the two terms and basic differences between them.

1. The mind is that which receives the external stimuli through sense organs and communicates the responses to the organs of action. Though the stimuli received through the five sense organs are distinct and different from one another, the mind is an integrated experience of them all. The intellect is the judging capacity, the discriminating and discerning faculty, which examines and judges the stimuli received by

the mind and communicates to the mind its decision on the type of responses to be executed. The mind is like a receiving and dispatching clerk, who mechanically receives the office mail and dispatches as per the instructions of the officer in-charge. The intellect may, therefore, be compared to the officer sitting in judgement over the disposal of papers received from his clerk and directing him as to the type of action to be taken. The mechanism of the mind and intellect and their functions are better understood with the help of an illustration. When an individual steps on a live cigarette he quickly removes his foot but before he does so, a series of reactions take place. As soon as the man's foot comes in contact with the fire, the skin carries the stimuli of heat to the mind, which, in turn, puts it up before the intellect for determining the type of reaction necessary. The intellect, with the help of the experience and knowledge gained by it in the past, orders the mind which in turn communicates the order to the muscles of the body to move the foot away since the object contacted is dangerous to the welfare of the individual.

2. Again, **mind is a continuous flow of thoughts.** If each thought is likened to a bucket of water, then the mind may be compared to a river, which is a constant flow of water. A bucket of water has no dynamism of its own, but, when many buckets of water continuously flow, the river gathers dynamism and

strength. So too, when thoughts flow continuously they cause a lot of agitation and the mind becomes the most powerful tyrant of man.

The intellect is the storehouse of all memory of one's past experiences and knowledge.This storehouse of experience is the guiding factor in man's actions. In the above simile, the intellect can be compared with the banks of a river, which determine its direction and course.

3. The mind can also be described as the seat of emotions and feelings and the intellect as the springboard of all ideas.

4. Another approach to the study of the mind and the intellect is to examine the realm in which they operate. The mind has a capacity to travel only to the 'realms known' but the intellect, besides remaining in the realms known, can further penetrate the 'realms unknown' to investigate, contemplate and comprehend new discoveries.

5. The mind and the intellect also differ in their nature and quality. The mind is ever in a state of flux. It is always the 'doubting element'. But **when the thoughts stabilize themselves to form a 'willed judgement' they are called the intellect.** For example when a man is indecisive as to whether he should be a vegetarian or non-vegetarian, his thoughts in that

condition of doubt and indecision are called the mind but when they take a firm decision, whatever it be, his thoughts acquire the status of intellect. Therefore, what is mind at one moment can be developed to an intellect at the next moment, and conversely an intellect can be reduced to the status of a mind when its decision is shattered by the suggestions of a more powerful intellect.

The above differentiation, meant for our clear understanding of the mind and intellect, is purely functional. In essence, however, they are both constituted of thoughts, and in the study of Vedānta, many a time either of them is used to indicate the other as well.

5. The Bliss Sheath

This is the innermost of the five sheaths consisting of vāsanās. It is made up of ignorance in which we exist during our deep-sleep state of consciousness. It is considered blissful, because whatever be the condition in which the individuals are in their waking and dream states, once they reach the halls of sleep, be they rich or poor, successful or disappointed, healthy or sick, young or old, all of them experience relatively the same undisturbed peace and bliss due to the cessation of agitation experienced by them in the other two states of consciousness. The Bliss Sheath controls the Intellectual Sheath, since the intellect functions under the control and guidance of one's vāsanās.

The synonyms for the Bliss Sheath are Vāsanās, Avidyā, Ignorance (of the Self), Non-apprehension (of Reality), Causal Body and the state of deep sleep. In a textbook of Vedānta these terms are so frequently used that knowledge of them becomes essential for our study. Although these are, in their essence, the same, each one is used to indicate a particular aspect of the same thing in a particular context.

The subtlest of all is the Ātman, which is the core of the five-sheath structure. The five sheaths are like the layers of clothes worn by a person, which are totally different from the wearer. So too, the Ātman is distinct and separate from the five matter-layers.

The Vital-air sheath is said to be 'within' the Food sheath and the Mental sheath 'within' the Vital-air sheath and so on; and the Ātman is the innermost. This may give us an idea that the Ātman is something very minute located inside the matter layers, which is contrary to the declaration of the Upaniṣads that it is all-pervading. The term 'within' has therefore, to be understood in the philosophical context in which it is used. When a sheath is said to be interior to another, it only indicates that the inner one is subtler than the outer. The subtler controls, regulates, feeds and nourishes the grosser. Hence the Ātman, which is the subtlest, is the controller and nourisher of all the five layers.

Again, **subtlety in philosophy is measured by pervasiveness;** for example, when a piece of ice melts, the water so formed occupies a larger area and hence we would, in philosophy say that water is subtler than ice. Also when the water is boiled, the steam generated spreads itself in the entire atmosphere of the room. Steam is, therefore, considered subtler than water.

Similarly, the Food sheath or the physical body is the grossest and it cannot expand more than perhaps a couple of inches around the waistline after a heavy meal. The Vital-air sheath consisting of the five prāṇas is more pervasive than the Food sheath since the perceptions go beyond the physical boundaries of the physical body. The mind is subtler still since it travels to realms (known only), which are beyond the area of perceptions and other physiological functions. The intellect, which has the capacity to travel even beyond the realms known and penetrates realms unknown, is obviously subtler than the mind. The vāsanās or the Bliss sheath is the subtlest of the five layers since it pervades all the above four layers and also independently in the state of deep sleep where none of the other layers has access.

The five sheaths have no separate existence as such; they are analysed only for our study.

The Food and the Vital-air sheaths together are called the gross body or sthūla śarira. The mental and intellectual sheaths together form the 'subtle body' or sukśma śarīra. The Bliss sheath is termed the 'causal body' or kāraṇa śarīra. The human structure can, therefore, be said to comprise the gross, subtle and causal bodies or the five sheaths enveloping the Consciousness or the Life Principle.

When the Consciousness, the Self within, identifies with the gross body, it expresses itself as the waker who enjoys the waking world and its experiences. The same Self, withdrawing from the gross body and identifying with the subtle body, manifests itself as the dreamer experiencing the dream world. Similarly, withdrawing from the gross and subtle bodies and identifying with the causal body, it functions as the deep sleeper who goes through a homogeneous experience of nothingness. This phenomenon is like an individual being called the father of his children, the officer in his office and the tennis player on the tennis court, though, in fact, these are only different names given to one and the same person without whom none of these manifestations are possible. So too, our real nature is the Pure Consciousness which transcends the three states of the waking, dream and deep sleep. It is because of the identification of the Self with the matter layers that the sorrows pertaining to the latter are superimposed on it.

Consider for example a tin containing an assortment of chocolates of different types, shapes and colours preserved in wrappers. A child, in its ignorance, chews the chocolate along with the silver paper wrapping. No doubt it enjoys the sweetness, but, the enjoyment is intercepted by the bitterness of the silver paper. So too, the Ātman is the Bliss Absolute, existing within the five layers of the matter but labelled as brahmin, non-brahmin, Indian, European etc., in the world. We the children of ignorance, try to enjoy Bliss along with the matter layers. Flickers of joy are, no doubt, experienced but they are followed by sorrow and bitterness. To experience the Absolute Bliss, therefore, we will have to analyse and discard the five layers of matter and apprehend the Self as different from the waker, dreamer and deep sleeper. This discrimination of the five superimposed layers of personality and recognition of one's own pure Self is termed Pañca-kośa-viveka.

The five kośas can also be classified under three categories as the gross, subtle and causal bodies which are the three vehicles in and through which the Self functions.

The world of objects, beings and happenings around man is not under his control. Disagreeable and painful events are bound to reach him time and again. But man alone has the capacity to control and regulate his reactions to such events and avoid getting adversely affected by them. In order to intelligently respond to them and gain happy experiences, he should know the equipment with which he has to face the incessant challenges of the world. Hence analysis and study of the kośas become essential for intelligent living

What is Ātman?

On an analysis of the human being, the Ṛṣis discovered that the five layers of personality are mere matter and that matter by itself is inert and insentient. Though constituted of matter, the individual is sentient and conscious of the world around him. It follows, therefore that there is in him something other than matter, which lends to it the sentiency or consciousness. This sentient or conscious principle is Ātman or God. It is like magnetism in a magnet, which is something other than the iron piece that it is.

The Ātman is that which gives the capacity to the sense organs to perceive, the mind to feel and the intellect to think. Hence it is often referred to in the śāstras as the perceiver, feeler and thinker on the physical, mental and intellectual planes respectively. It is likened to electricity, which manifests differently through different equipment.

Hence, **the Ātman is indicated as something other than the gross, subtle and causal bodies, beyond the five sheaths of matter; a witness to the waking, dream and deep sleep states of consciousness and the perceiver in the** sense organs, **feeler in the mind and the thinker in the intellect.**

Total field of objects perceived	]
+	] The World
Total emotions felt	] experienced by an
+	] individual (OET)
Total thoughts entertained	]
Perceiver	]
+	] The Ego
Feeler	] or
+	] Individuality (PFT)
Thinker	]
Body+Mind+Intellect	- The equipment of
	the individual (BMI)

The gross body contains the five organs of perception (the eyes, the ears, the nose, the tongue and the skin) and the five organs of action (the hands, the legs, speech, genital organ and the organ of evacuation). It is the medium through which the individual contacts the outer world of objects and experiences his joys or sorrows.

The subtle body is made up of the mental and intellectual sheaths, which respectively contain emotions and feelings of the mind and ideas and ideals of the intellect. All these are mere thoughts. The subtle body, is, therefore, constituted of thoughts just as gold ornaments are made up of gold or mud pots of mud.

However, there are functional differences in these thoughts, which have given them four distinct status known as:

Mind, Manas
Intellect, Buddhi
Ego, Ahaṅkāra
Memory, Citta

These four put together constitute our inner equipment, Antaḥkaraṇa, in contrast to the outer equipment, Dasa-indriyas i.e. the ten organs of the body. The four are only functional names for the same basic substance, namely, thoughts.

Manas

In an experience, the first impact of stimuli through the organs of perception causes disturbance in the thought and there is restlessness and indecision. This condition of doubt or indecision of the thought is called the mind – Sankalpa-Vikalpātmakam Manaḥ.

Buddhi

After the first impact, the disturbance dies down and there is quietude of decision and determination. This condition of decision of thought is called the intellect – niścayātmika buddhiḥ.

Ahaṅkāra

A doubt and a decision will be related to each other only if they belong to a single individual. When both of them reside in a person, he is aware that the doubt and the decision are 'His'. The constant concept of 'I-ness' in his feelings of 'doubt' and 'I decide' is also a thought and its functional name is ego – Ahaṅkartā Ahaṅkāraḥ.

Citta

The fourth aspect of the subtle body is the Citta. Citta is the thought-forms of the nature of memory.

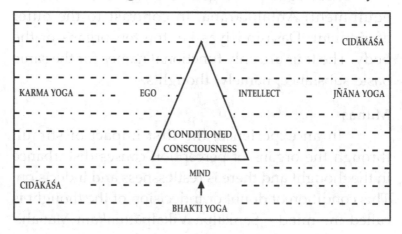

Cidākāsa

Cidākāsa is the unconditioned consciousness, which is all-pervading.

The seeker sees himself as the conditional Consciousness presently. The sādhanās of bhakti, karma and jñāna make him realize that he is unconditioned Consciousness.

When the mind, intellect and ego are eliminated, the conditioned consciousness merges with the unconditioned Pure Consciousness. For example, the sunlight in a room, which is conditioned by the walls of the room, merges with the sunlight outside when the walls are broken down. Similarly, the conditioned Consciousness merges with Cidākāsa by breaking the wall of the mind through the path of devotion or bhakti-yoga, by breaking the wall of the intellect through the path of knowledge or jñāna-yoga, and the wall of the ego through the path of action or karma-yoga. When any one of the three viz. mind, intellect or ego is eliminated, all the three get eliminated since they are all made up of the same substance viz. thoughts. What remains thereafter, is pure objectless Awareness – The Cidākāsa .

The essential nature of man is Absolute Knowledge; so, when intellect fails to apprehend a thing, the mind refuses to accept its non-apprehension and instead, starts misinterpreting and creating a false unreal projection upon the object. This is illustrated in the analogy of the post and ghost – sthānu-puruṣa.

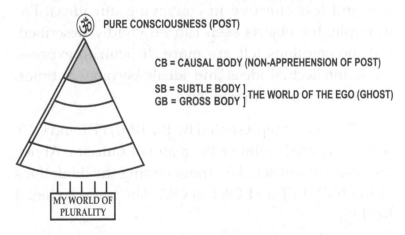

PURE CONSCIOUSNESS (POST)

CB = CAUSAL BODY (NON-APPREHENSION OF POST)

SB = SUBTLE BODY]
GB = GROSS BODY] THE WORLD OF THE EGO (GHOST)

MY WORLD OF PLURALITY

In the analogy, a man mistakes a post for a ghost. The non-apprehension of the post is the root cause of the misapprehension that it is the ghost. This illusion of the ghost can never be removed except by gaining the knowledge or apprehension of the post.

Similarly, by the non-apprehension of the reality (avidyā), the intellect is veiled (āvaraṇa) and the mind is agitated (vikṣepa). Consequently, the mind projects mis-apprehensions on the Reality and identifying itself with them gives rise to the world of plurality. This phenomenon of projection and identification of the mind is called superimposition. With the dawn of knowledge, avidyā or ignorance is removed and the concept of the pluralistic world vanishes leaving the supreme Reality.

In our day-to-day experiences, we find that as the subject gets subtler and subtler, language becomes less and less effective in conveying our ideas. For example, the objects seen can be vividly described, but the emotions felt are more difficult to express, while intellectual ideas and ideals become, at times, almost impossible to convey.

The world represented by the BMI, PFT and OET is the terrestrial realm or the realm of saṁsāra. Above the realm of saṁsāra i.e., transcending the limitations of the BMI, PFT and OET is OM, The transcendental Reality.

Language is useful only to express the ideas pertaining to the terrestrial realm but when employed to express the transcendental, it proves a failure unless it is manipulated and scaffolded with words having deep suggestive import. Hence we find that, scriptural language is cryptic and not easy to understand; we require preceptors to interpret and explain the scriptures.

Saṁskṛt is the language, which has gone through purification and preparation and has been successfully employed by the great Ṛṣis to indicate as best as possible the inexpressible.

Philosophy in India has sprung from the spiritual experiences of the ancient sages; it is not the result of mere intellectual speculation. Since it aims at the knowledge of the transcendental Reality, it is termed Darśana, or vision of Truth in saṁskṛt . Every Indian school of philosophy holds, in its own way, that there is a direct realization of Truth. A man of realization enjoys total liberation from the strains, stresses and limitation of the terrestrial realm; one who fails to attain realization is entangled in them and is lost.

Vedānta stands out as the clearest and most significant native philosophy of India. It answers at once strict demands of metaphysics and the deep requirements of a sound religion. However the system of Vedānta derives its doctrine from the Prasthāna-

Traya, which comprises the three textbooks viz., The Upaniṣads, the Bhagavad-gītā and the Brahma-sūtras. Vedānta is the clearest and most comprehensive summary ever made of the perennial philosophy; hence its enduring value is meant not only for Indians, but also for all the mankind.

The quintessence of the Vedānta philosophy is found in the great declarations (Mahāvākyas) of the four Vedas. These are ranged in the following ascending order:

1. Prajñānam Brahma(Consciousness is Brahman).
2. Tat Tvam Asi (That Thou Art).
3. Ayam Ātma Brahma (This Self is Brahman).
4. Aham Brahma Asmi. (I am Brahman).

The first Mahāvākya gives an objective definition of Truth. It declares that the Consciousness, the spiritual core that makes one's personality layers dynamic and active, is the Consciousness that pulsates in all beings and pervades everywhere.

The second Mahāvākya is addressed by a master to a disciple, after having defined that Brahman is Consciousness. He declares the greatest Truth "That Thou Art"; Oh! Disciple that Brahman which is nothing but Consciousness, is not yonder in the clouds to be achieved as a posthumous reward, but it is right here and now, to be experienced as the Ātman within your own self.

After hearing the definition of Brahman and after having understood from the words of his Master that he is, in essence, nothing other than Brahman, the seeker retires to a quiet place, shut off from worldly cares, to meditate upon the objective truth that "Self is Consciousness". Ere long he realises that "The Self is Brahman". Having decided for himself from his own personal solitary and tranquil meditation that this Ātman is Brahman, the student comes back to the master and, to the looks of enquiry of the master, answers with the cheer that beams out of his limpid eyes of peace and serenity, that he had intimately experienced the Truth and he is living with the constant awareness of the Truth – "I am Brahman".

Thus, in the first two Mahāvākyas we find the definition of Truth and the relationship between Truth and man. The other two give us an assurance that Truth is realised not partially but totally.

Philosophy, therefore, explains the mysteries of man and the universe. It points out the unseen string that holds together the heterogeneous phenomenon – it makes man understand, what he is now, and what he should really be. It gives him the key to open the kingdom of heaven that lies within. Philosophy bridges the gulf between the man and God.

However, **philosophy is only a view of life, while religion is a way of life.** Philosophy without religion, is tantamount to a utopian myth; religion divorced from philosophy becomes a bundle of superstitions.

Religion is the science of self-purification; it is a means to an end. Religion, as is manifest from the derivation of the term (re=back and ligare=to bind) is that which binds one back to the original or fountainhead. Therefore, **by understanding the word 'religion', we can come to the conclusion that any technique by which, man regains his original glory is religion.**

Religion is, therefore, not mere ritual, though rites play an important role in the religious scheme of mental integration and self-purification. A man, whose mind and intellect are well integrated will, by practicing various religious techniques, seek ere long the identity with the Self, the Truth. This merger of the little self (ego) with the Real Self (Ātman) is indeed the goal of religion.

The word yoga comes from the root yuj=join. So, **yoga means the joining of the ego to the Supreme Self.** While the final merger is the fulfilment of the yoga, even the techniques which promote one's progress towards the realisation of the Supreme are called yoga. Thus, there are, in Hinduism, four paths to reach the ultimate goal. They are:

1. Bhakti-yoga – The Path of Devotion.
2. Jñāna-yoga – The Path of Knowledge.

3. Karma-yoga – The Path of Action.

4. Hatha-yoga – The Path of Mysticism.

Even though the techniques are different, the goal reached by all these paths is one and the same, and the main scientific theory in these techniques is based upon mental integration and self-purification, even in the rules of life laid down for the practitioner. Thus there is uniformity; and yet, there are many paths given to us to accommodate the different temperaments and types of individuals.

24. LIFE IS YOURS – KINDLE IT

The indifference to religion of the apparently educated man of today is not so much due to the futility or hollowness of the science of the religion as such, but his own incapacity to understand the textbooks of religion in the world. This is true not only of the Hindu but also of men of every faith. This difficulty in accommodating the old ideas to the news of thinking, is felt by the faithful of all the established religions all over the globe.

True religion never dies; Hinduism is not dead. If on the wayside we find the extending branches of a dry tree, naked of leaves and flowers, it is possible that in our hurry, we may consider that to be the skeleton of a dead tree that was once gloriously alive. Now, however, it spreads no shadow and protects but a few pilgrims under its thin shade. And yet, a lover of trees who knows the art of farming discovers some parasites flourishing on the withered tree. The sight of this parasitic growth is sufficient for the scientist to have a vision of the sap that runs in the core of the seemingly dead tree. He need not cut the trunk down to see if the sap is still running.

Similarly, Hinduism is proving today that it has no widespreading shadow to shelter the whole community; bereft of its leafy roof, it has the inauspicious look of some grinning skeleton in the sepulchre. But since the great Hindu tree continues to nourish and maintain many a parasitic growth, a true cultivator of religion takes heart and cries "This is not dead. The sap is still running. This can be revived".

Just as the farmer, in reviving the dead tree, would ruthlessly remove the parasites, intelligently cut down the unnecessary burden of its extending branches, loosen the soil at the roots, and nourish it with regular supplies of fresh soil and food, so too, the tree of our religion can be redeemed, trimmed, and revitalized with the nourishing salt of understanding, and the true waters of sincere seeking.

Then, shall the children of the present discover, through a thorough study of our ancient scriptures, that modern science and ancient religion are not such strangers as they assume them to be. When I say religion, I do not claim for it an application only to Hinduism; it is as much true of Hinduism as of any other religion in the world today, Unfortunately we have come to identify the term 'religion', with stony edifices of temples and mosques, churches and synagogues, pagodas and gurudwaras, with different sacred books, endless and varying interpretations, confusing rituals, and in their name, painful mutual quarrels, resulting in hatred and violence. This is often the result of the colossal ignorance of what is true religion.

Religion is to be understood essentially as a science of living so that we may cull out of it a set of desirable values of life, upon which we can rebuild wisely our day-to-day existence. If the existing religion is too old, outmoded and obsolete, and if the fundamental values of life preached by it cannot solve our day's problems, we shall without regret discard the whole lot and strive to discover new principles and laws of right living. If religion is but a dictatorial declaration of a scheme of living, which has no reference at all to our day-to-day existence, and cannot solve our pressing problems, we shall banish the old religion and take to a new culture and a more desirable cult; for man is, and should be, primarily concerned with his life here, rather than in the hereafter.

It may be reasonably be asked "Why should a man hunt after the knowledge of a greater Reality, of a greater power behind the obvious, the perceived, the experienced world of senses?" In fact, we find there is no institution called religion among the animals. The necessity for religion, the urge for spiritual freedom, the call from the depths within ourselves, is experienced only by man, and even then, it is not felt by all men. In every generation, it is inevitable that a significant minority should feel a thirst for enquiring into this great Reality. Why a glorious minority alone comes to feel the urge to face this vital problem, has been exhaustively dealt with in our old texts and has been vaguely hinted at by Darwin in his theory of evolution. He seems to explain to us that life, though it started as an accident, went on multiplying and developing into the various levels of evolutions, to reach its cumulative achievement in the 'thinking being' called man. Therefore, Darwin suddenly rockets up all his readers into a utopian joy, with this optimistic promise, that evolution will still continue to accomplish itself in a generation of supermen!

If this biologist prophet were true in his conclusions, we have to accept that the ape or ape-man somehow lost his tail and started daily shaving to become the man of today. Thus, from the animal kingdom, evolution extended itself to flourish in the achievements of a full-grown man. But here again, has obviously been a period of transition wherein we find beings of animalistic instinct in the form of men, behaving and acting as though they were not better than mere animals. For these beings, which live through the equipment of the animal, though men in shape and form, it is hardly possible to rise above the values entertained by the animal kingdom. To them, religion cannot have direct or immediate appeal at all.

But, to those who have long since, passed this stage and have grown through the vicissitudes of life into beings better developed mentally and intellectually, challenging questions begin to pose themselves: **"From where did all these things come? Where do they go and why? Is there a mission and purpose in life or is life a mere accident?"**

To these developed beings, religion has a meaning, and a purpose, and shows the path and the goal. No religion is possible in the world without a philosophy, and philosophy always tries to explain to us, the world in which we live, and the causes for the same. Here indeed is a fundamental difference between the concepts of philosophy entertained in the east and in the west!

Extrovert by nature, philosophy to the westerner, is to a great extent an objectified science. To them, philosophy points out **a view of life**. The ideal may, and does often change, with the result, that we have a new ideal in the West almost every decade!

In the East, philosophy means something more than an attempt to show a view of life, for, the Āryans were the most practical of men. They demanded that the ideas and ideals preached by the philosopher should be capable of being practised, and so, every philosopher was compelled not only to paint a glorious picture of the ideal world, but also to give the topography and the route to it in all detail. Thus, **to the East, philosophy was not only a view of life but, a way of life as well!**

The philosophy pointing out the view of life can certainly be scientific, but it would lack the technique; and science without a technique, is a mere fable for children to read. With this point of view in mind, when we try to investigate into the religions of the world, we shall find that of all the existing religions, Hinduism, in its Vedāntic philosophy, supplies us with not only a mere enumeration of the enduring foundations upon which a peaceful world of progressive living can be organized, but also an eminently satisfactory line of argument to establish why those values are absolute and fundamental!

25. VEDĀNTA–LIFE AND ART OF LIVING

Our age has been branded as atheistic and secular because we dare to question and we do so openly. We are not prepared to swallow any declaration; however great the prophet may be or however revered the sage may be, unless it is convincingly proved to our vigilant reason as satisfactorily logical. We claim to live in an age of perfect intellectual awareness and scientific precision. Faith has the least hold on us; but if the arguments are intellectual and scientific, we can be made to slave cheerfully under a tyrant or even walk on our heads.

This being the tendency of the age, the philosophy of Vedānta as expounded in the Upaniṣads holds for us a compelling charm. Comparing Hinduism with any other religion in the world, wherein religion is guided by the airtight declaration of a given prophet or master, it can be defined as a 'Growing tradition'. Like modern science, Hinduism is not the declaration of any one individual, but is the conclusion of generations of investigators.

Even at this moment, scientific conclusions are changeable, and many have in fact changed when reviewed in the light of newly discovered data. Similarly, in religion too, though the fundamentals remain the same, their application in life changes from time to time according to the changing demand of an ever-growing society. In this sense, a scripture that allows no freedom to expand, will only choke itself and society, just as an iron casket is hardly a healthy shelter around the growing girth of a gigantic tree. Vedānta seems to have so far historically served all the growing demands of men.

Unfortunately, the moment we hear the word Vedānta , there are many critics who are reminded of Ācārya Śaṅkara and other commentators and they roll up their noses expecting endless controversial discussions and fanatic assertions. The modern educated young men, in their hasty conclusion, generally come to a feeling, and I was myself one of them, that the ideas preached in Vedānta are the moaning and sobs of some strange type of men who gained strange view; based upon some miscalculations. They were supposed to suffer from psychological perversions; produced by their unnatural life of seclusion in the jungle, during the days of self-denial and self-courted sufferings.

But a little scientific scrutiny will reveal that these Ṛṣis exhibited no greater stranger peculiarity in their behaviour and life than that of any genius of the present day. For example, watch a scientist, a poet, a painter,

109

or a musician. If he be a genius in his life, completely dedicated to his work, if he be one who seeks his life's fulfilment in his chosen pursuit, we shall find that he does not subscribe himself to the commonly accepted traditions of living or behaviour. He is so engrossed in his work that he has, as it were, no eyes to see others, no ears to hear anything else, no personality even to demand any of his fundamental rights, apart from his freedom to pursue his sacred vocation. The idiosyncrasies of the artists, the absentmindedness of the professor, the self-centred preoccupations of the thinkers... these are the common hallmarks of a single minded devotion to a particular ideal.

In this sense, if we try to understand the Ṛṣis as true scientists of living, we will realize that their solitude and detachment are the unavoidable necessities of their sacred vocation. In his perfect detachment, the Ṛṣis observed life and analysed and reached certain conclusions. These conclusions were faithfully transferred to a set of his disciples initially, trained to use the instruments of the mind and intellect, to make independent valuations of life as a whole. They were also taught to work out accurately its effect on individual persons under different sets of circumstances.

All through these experiments, all of them recognized that the one unavoidable factor in life is that none can continue living life without experience, since life is merely a continuity of experiences. The moment the individual has stopped experiencing anything within or without, he is considered to be dead. Thereafter, decay sets in and the form and structure of the person crumbles down to become the very elements of which it was constituted.

In every experience, man yearns to gain the perfection; he wants happiness and peace. Perfect peace and endless happiness satisfy him. Thus, seeking new occasions to experience a more perfect and more complete happiness, he goes from one set of circumstances to another created by changing the arrangement of things; all in the hope that he may procure for himself a greater and better happiness, fuller and deeper.

Whatever be the type of experience we may gain, it is certain that an experience can be gained only when we come across the world of the 'experienced'. **The greater the understanding of the world of objects, the better shall be our relationship with it.** With that right understanding if we approach the world, it shall yield for us a fuller satisfaction and with lesser chances of disillusionment and despairs. The thesis that Vedānta propounds is that in our hasty, unintelligent evaluation of life, of things and beings, we have always made a wrong estimate of the world; by superimposing false values of things, we have come to suffer the consequent imperfections in our experiences. This pale vision of a misinterpreted world, which naturally doles out to us our ample share of sorrows, is fully condemned by the wise seers in the Upaniṣads. They make a passionate appeal to man to make a right re-estimate of the world of objects.

It is in this sense that Vedānta declares, "The world is unreal, the Truth (Brahman) is the only Reality." Therefore, if understood properly, Vedānta only demands of us a healthier re-interpretation of the world. The calumny that is generally thrown at the doors of Vedānta, that it admonishes us to be indifferent to the sorrows of man, to social injustice, to poverty and slavery, is an unjust criticism made by those who are interested in this blasphemy. They are applauded only by the gullible and the ignorant.

Religion is not the personal property of an individual or an institution. Properly understood, it is not a set of declarations made by some strange men with rare powers of vision or some bundles of mysterious rituals, or some secret den of ominous conspiracies. On the contrary, it is a complete science of perfect living, whereby society can learn to live peacefully and fully.

There was a time when religion chose not to recognize science and refused to shake hands with her and this almost prepared religion's own grave. Today, we find the same mistake repeated in the opposite camp. Science has deliberately and openly disowned religion, and consequently materialism, at the height of its perfection, is groaning with the sorrows of its own creation. Neither of them can stand on its own if it wants to bring happiness to society and serve man in living his daily life.

In fact, the principles of science and the scientific approach vitalize religion. Similarly, the achievements in productions, the efficiency in distribution, the gains of cooperation, the marvels of discoveries, the victory over nature, etc., cannot in themselves meet the demands of life, and assure a greater share of human happiness. These should be backed by the practice of nobler values of healthy living, preached by religion. The individuals constituting the community, should also strictly pursue the teachings of self-integration.

A community or a nation is, we should not forget, constituted of its members and the strength of the nation or the happiness of the community depends not only upon the material gains or the peculiar pattern of the circumstances in life, but also upon the structure and composition of the individuals themselves. We can, with knowledge of architecture, make easily a perfect blueprint for the most magnificent edifice in the world, but in its construction, unless we are careful of the quality of the bricks used, the edifice will soon entomb all the inhabitants who take shelter within its accommodation. Similarly, the secular plans and scientific knowledge of this materialistic age are certainly magnificent on paper and in theory, but all of them seem to crumble into nothingness, and entomb our happiness, when they are put into practice. This has been the repeated experience of our materialistic civilization. History records it; our own experiences endorse it in no uncertain terms.

The redemption seems to be in the happy marriage between the secular and the sacred, the scientific and the religious. So far, the scientist, pure and simple, has failed to establish a scheme of living by which man can attain a peaceful and joyous way of existence. The history of man has been a melancholy story of repeated wars and revolutions, all fought in the name of peace. In its sacred name, we have learnt to take weapons of destruction and kill each other with ruthless efficiency!!! The peace that we know of today is but the exhausting, fatiguing, demoralizing pause between two immediate wars. After every spasm of cruelty and bloodshed, the animal in us, in sheer exhaustion, seeks a shelter wherein to mourn or to roll upon itself until it licks it wounds dry and gets ready to fight again!

All the lovely wars and revolutions have not succeeded in discovering that secret prescription for joy, or that system of perfect government where each citizen can bloom forth into the maximum happiness he is capable of. This failure can directly be traced to the very ignorance in us, of the real meaning of life, and its component parts. It is forgotten or not realized at all that the external pattern of objects cannot and will not consistently remain long in any given scheme, formulated through the pen, the word or the sword. The pattern changes eternally and so do the minds of individuals. In this welter of change, to maintain equilibrium is a utopian dream. Thus, all revolutionary changes for a congenial living pattern are necessarily endeavours doomed to failure, so long as they ignore the subject unit, constituted of the mental, the intellectual and the spiritual personalities of man.

Then, is philosophy a dream of despair? If it were so, man would have long ago thrown it overboard and got himself relieved from its severe implications. On the other hand, true philosophy is the most optimistic call to man, to act diligently and wisely, carving out for himself, from moment to moment, a greater state of perfection, whereby he can come to live in a fuller world of nobler endeavours, pursuing the more enduring values.

The solution, which our seers have offered to the world, seems to be a call, to accomplish this inner revolution. According to them, the true goal of joy can be reached only if the mind and intellect of the individuals are controlled, and patterned, so as to find for themselves their equipoise in all the changing vicissitudes of life. They have minutely described the strategies to be followed, and the methods to be adopted, to achieve this inner transformation. Their aim was in fact to discover the fundamental and the absolute reality in life.

It took them many a century of minute observation, patient analysis, and laborious recording to discover that an experience consists of three fundamental factors, viz.:

i. The Subject : The Experiencer
ii. The Object : The Experienced and
iii.The relationship between the
subject and the object : The Experiencing

Where any of these three is absent, an experience cannot come to pass, just as in the absence of any one of the three components of the atom, it must necessarily, disintegrate.

In this combination of the experiencer, the experienced and the experiencing, it is evident that the secular scientists chose for themselves the field of the 'experienced' for their investigation and achievement while the subtle scientists of life of the Ṛṣis, took up for their field of enquiry the world of the experiencer. Thus, the difference between the secular scientists and the Ṛṣis lay only in this, that while the former were seekers of truth, working in the outer field of the material objects, the latter chose the inner world of the subjects and through it the all-pervading Truth.

These subjective thinkers found, in the course of their observations, that when a subject comes across an object and earns for himself an experience, **the experiencer, though he be physically one, becomes a composite structure of four different personalities: the physical, the psychological, the intellectual and the spiritual**. The various subtle aspects of his reaction make him so! They are so subtle and at the moment of experiencing them all work so quickly that the superficial observer fails to recognize the fine distinction in this simultaneous action.

Their laborious experiments and exhaustive reports crystallize for us the clear theory, that, when a subject comes into contact with an object, it does so, not as an integrated whole but with four distinct mouths as it were, from the four different layers in the person. Four differently constituted entities, each having its own demands and values, rise up at the challenge of every situation created by any object or being, and thrust at once to experience it.

Suppose a cake has been offered by your neighbours as a casual present to you. The physical man in you at once jumps up to experience it, the eyes registering its shape, the nose its smell, the skin its touch- and perhaps the tongue, as a result, even starts watering. The mental man in you also rushes forth to experience it, but it decides that it can enjoy the cake better after a couple of hours, since it is not very hungry. Nor is this all. The intellectual faculty in you, may also rise up to evaluate the situation and may be it will remember the warning of the doctor that cake is bad for your body since you are diabetic. Further, the sense of the divine, the conception of the truth in you, may create a hesitation in accepting the cake from the neighbour and putting yourself under an acquaintance's obligation!

Thus, at every moment, in each of our experiences, four different processes as it were, protrude from us to suck at the situation and earn a synthetic profit of the experiences. When the four different powers behaving as unacquainted strangers from different realms, each entertaining different values of life, come together to enjoy any given subject or situation, invariably, that which brings satisfaction to one, conveys but varying degrees of dissatisfaction to all the other three. **Consequently, no situation has yet been discovered by an ordinary mortal in whom he can seek and hope to discover a complete satisfaction for all the 'four' in him.**

In this scheme of existence, in this confusion of personalities within ourselves, in this tragic chaos within, man's attempt at peace and tranquillity, his endless ambition to gain joy and perfection, his hope to live in smiles and cheers should necessarily get blasted and push him into a chasm of despair, despondency, dejection and disquiet. In short, the inner chaos of the personalities in him is the unseen cause of all the sorrows of life, called by the familiar term saṁsāra.

The sensitive masters of old must have also felt the desperate straits, into which man is thrown by circumstances, and they soon discovered a method, by which man could efficiently and faithfully integrate the four entities in him into one synthetic whole, so that this integrated 'four in one' personality may find a conducive happiness in itself, wherein any part in it finds itself in a satisfactory scheme of joy if a chariot is drawn by four vicious horses, each in its wild strength pulling it in a different direction, the unharnessed powers will not allow it down the embankment; so too, today, inwardly disintegrated as we are in our pilgrimage of life, we are getting ourselves wrecked on the wayside ditches, progressing nowhere towards our goal!

The practical proposition of religion is a theory that propounds how we can train the 'four' in us, and make a pleasant joyride through the avenues of our appointed life. The practical suggestions and the exercises recommended by religion contain in their respective ritualistic activities, all the known scientific methods by which, each one of us can get ourselves fully and completely integrated. The greater the integration, the greater is our freedom from the thraldom of life. Indeed, it would be a consummate achievement if we truly gain a perfect freedom from the external world of ever-changing experiences, and discover for ourselves a balance and tranquillity that is permanent and unchangeable.

The Technique of Self-Development

During their investigations into the structure of the experiencer, the Ṛṣis of yore, not only discovered that there are four different entities in each experiencer, but also found that every man comes to make a ready sacrifice of the grosser, in preference to the subtler in him.

This can be illustrated by a simple example. If you are required to make a physical sacrifice for the sake of one who is an acquaintance, you will be loath to make that sacrifice. But if there be a boil or an ulcer on any of your limbs which causes you infinite pain, you would not hesitate to rush to a doctor and on his advice sacrifice that limb through an amputation, if need be. When you come to the realm of the intellect, you will find that for the sake of intellectual satisfaction you may be ready to sacrifice even the body. Of such stuff were the martyrs in history made. Political history has shown, that when man is intellectually fired by some convincing ideas, he is prepared to suffer any amount of physical and mental sufferings in order to achieve the objective.

Thus, psychological satisfaction is richer than physical gratification; the subtler the personality, the greater is the satisfaction that is derived by the individual and while identifying with the subtler in us, we readily get ourselves transcended from the world of the grosser and its joys and sorrows. If this is a scientific fact, then is there any method by which all of us can identify ourselves with the subtlest in us and try to live in the world continuously in that state?

This pursuit led the Vedic seers to plan technical methods by which the integration of the personality can effectively take place and with the help of which self-transcendence can easily be achieved. They did strive by these methods to bring about a better constituted society of dynamic men, healthy in body, cheerful in mind, strong in intellect and firm in spirit. Love and ambition were the compulsion that made them work for human redemption and therefore, they did not incorporate any idea of their own, however noble, unless it was completely practical and would suit every individual in the world. So universal was their conception that their theories and practices are applicable to all ages and to all geographical spheres.

Just as Physics, Biology, etc. are not the exclusive property of any one country or people, of an era or an age, but are universally applicable irrespective of time and age, so too, the science of living as propounded by the Ṛṣis in Vedānta visualizes a plan of life to suit all people at all times and everywhere.

Since the theory is universally applicable and the technique suits the psychological composition of different ages and groups, they in their sacred wisdom realized that a limited castiron pattern couldn't hold everyone for all times. Between man and man, there is a clear distinction both in their individual mental attitude and intellectual grasp. As such, a set scheme to control and develop the mind and intellect for all people would be an impracticable proposition and an absurdity too colossal for their wisdom to even contemplate.

It is an accepted fact that life, considered as a series of experiences, is enjoyed mainly by our 'head and heart' i.e., the rational and intellectual faculty represented by the head and the faculty of instinct and emotion represented by the heart. If these two factors control and regulate, order and dictate the texture of our experience, and if there be such an endless diversity in experiences between man and man, then, it must be because of the varying proportion in which 'the head and the heart' function in the different individuals. Therefore, on the basis of these two factors, the entire humanity may be satisfactorily divided into four types:

1. Those in whom the 'Heart' predominates over the 'Head'.

2. Those in whom the 'Head' predominates over the 'Heart'.
3. Those in whom the 'Head' and the ' Heart' have an almost equal assertion.
4. Those in whom neither the 'Head' nor the 'Heart' has developed adequately.

This classification is built upon the basis of comparative assertions of the emotional and the rational traits in man and upon his estimation of things and situations during his endless experiencing of the world. For, there is no one who is the purely intellect type or the purely heart type.

In this perplexity, if the science of self-integration had only one airtight method, it could save only a small fraction of the entire population. Thus, the existing religions of the world, when compared with inimitable perfection of Hinduism, are all imperfect in themselves to become a universal religion, for all times and for all people. This is no fault of theirs, nor is it a reflection on the prophets. It is only the result of a limitation, germane to a single immortalized mortal who comes for a time, to address his generation. The anxiety of the prophets was the redemption of their generation from the particular weakness of the age, and as such, each religion had a special justification for that particular age, since it served to solve the immediate problems of that generation. It would, therefore, be ridiculous and most absurd to insist with fanatical emphasis that the same religion should be applied in all its entirety, with ruthless bigotry, to all people and at all times.

But, the exhaustive treatment as it is available for us in the literature of the Hindu scriptures, seems to consider the entire problem of man and successfully serves in pursuing all his possibilities. Therefore, **Hinduism can serve all people at all times**. However, the scientific method should be, in its application to the new problems, related from time to time, to suit the spirit of the new age and society. It is merely a question of shifting the emphasis from one aspect to another, which is determined by the weakness in the mental and intellectual life of the people. This is the secret of the survival of Hinduism from out of its many dark ages and in spite of its repeated destiny to live under unsympathetic governments in its own native land.

Yet, unfortunately, many a Hindu, ignorant or worse still ill-educated vanity of his misdirected education and ill-digested knowledge seems to feel that the different paths for self-development available in our literature are themselves its very weakness. We are reminded of a story, wherein a beggar who was allowed to use a king's palace, complained of the inconveniences which the palace with its innumerable rooms and halls provided for him. The modern Hindu condemns his religion, because it is so exhaustive. Ignorance alone can parade such shameless audacity.

In order to serve the four different types, mentioned above, the scientists of life, desirous of helping to gain for everyone a complete integration of his individual personality, prescribed four distinct methods, which have come down to us as the four yoga traditions; devotion or bhakti; knowledge or jñāna; selfless-work or karma; and the mystic way or hatha-yoga.

Of these four methods, bhakti is the path that can serve the majority of the people all over the world at all times, since man is essentially a creature of emotions and sentiments, of impulses and attachments. For this reason, we find that in almost all the religions of the world the emphasis is on the path of devotion and rarely, if at all, do we find people believing that selfless work also can be conducive to self-development. We may safely say that the mystical path and the path of pure knowledge are the exclusive techniques which the incomparable genius of the Ṛṣis alone could have given to the world.

Bhakti or the path of devotion is, most appealing to the generality of mankind, especially to those who have the sad experience of unrewarded love, unappreciated kindness and unrequited sympathies. An emotional creature cannot feel happy, unless its emotions are in chorus sung back. Where there is no emotional echo, there the psychological satisfaction stops to throb; choked by its own unrewarded emotions it gets strangled by the sweetness of its own sentiments. Such an individual finds an ample field for loving the Lord, who, in Himself, represents the ideal of inexhaustible love, infinite kindness and endless sympathy. When a devotee thus directs his entire mental energies towards this infinite ocean of love, all the love that he can gain comes to be but a drop compared with that Prem-sāgar which his ideal represents. Thus, the individual comes to feel a consummate fulfilment in loving the Lord of his heart, who never deserts him, but shows His love and kindness even through life's sorrows, and bereavements, disappointments and dejection, despair and despondency.

To the man of 'head' this method can hardly have any appeal, for, to him, emotion has no secret meaning. He can enjoy emotion only when it is sanctioned and acknowledged by his reason. He demands satisfaction for the "head'; and he views and evaluates things from the crown of his intellect. The soft silk clad, bejewelled and bedecked flute player, or the rag clad, bearded cross bearer, is to the purely intellectual, a mere mental, who might have achieved perfection in his day, yet is but a finite specimen as much limited in space and time as any one of us. To an individual who entertains such an idea, the path of devotion is no inspiring avenue to gain any amount of self-integration. Perhaps, if he is forced to walk the path through social pressure or through fear of unhealthy criticism, he only wrecks himself and ends by becoming a much more disintegrated brute than what he was, when he walked into the church or the temple.

To cater to such men, nowhere in the world can we find a satisfactory philosophy or even a sufficiently subtle method except in the Vedānta. Aldous Huxley represents in large measure the above type.

Vedānta recognizes so freely the potentialities of the human intellect that the children of the modern scientific age stand aghast at their own incapacity to live up to its full destiny and to make use of their entire birthright by completely exerting their individual intellect in the pursuit of seeking the good and the perfect. Those who cry out aloud that religion is empty and hollow, that it is a bundle of empty superstitious beliefs, that it insults our intellectual assertion, are those who have not been initiated into the sacred freedom which Vedānta liberally gives to the intelligent. Through pure reason one climbs the path of Vedānta and it ultimately leads us to discriminate between the permanent and the ephemeral, between the real and the unreal, between the false and the true in ourselves, and make us rediscover ourselves, to be the true, the real and the permanent. Godhood is the goal of Vedānta and in it lies the glory of Hinduism. This too, is the path of those who seek reality through knowledge or jñāna.

To serve men of mixed psychology who seesaw between the cooing of their heart and the call of their intellect, the karma or the path of action has been advised. Here, the individual during his softer moments of emotional desperation walks the path of devotion while during his intellectual phase he runs out into the field of activity to serve society as a manifestation of the Lord of his heart.

A selfless worker is not a psychological wreck who has split his potentialities on the rock of idle anxieties over the plans of action or in futile hopes of expected fruits or imagined results. To him the very field of activity is an expression of Lord's kindness and his only demand in life is that he may be a true instrument of the Lord in fulfilling His plans among His creations. The very feeling of His blessing flowing through the devotee is sufficient reward, a thrilling divine experience for him, and a selfless worker refuses to demand anything more from his Lord. This satisfies both changing tides of the 'head' and the 'heart' in the individual belonging to this composite type of personality.

Those who belong to the last group, who have comparatively maladjusted or ill-formed 'head' and 'heart' would have been the despair of every prophet and no religion in the world could prescribe for them a treatment and a path by which they could complete their biological evolution and walk the path of the spirit towards self-redemption.

The acute intelligence, the highly evolved scientific knowledge of living creatures and their structure, the divinely sweet temperament of love and charity, the Godly urge to serve even the dullest- these whipped the Godman in the Vedic period to devise a subtle method of physical exercises. This is a system of conscious self-control by which such an individual can slowly be awakened, first to the full stature of man, and thereafter be guided out of the labyrinth of his own misunderstandings to the sunny fields of self-discovery and infinite perfection. The technique prescribed is called hatha-yoga, which comprises the special exercises, which popularly go by the names āsana and prāṇāyāma.

With open eyes and wide awakened intelligence these Ṛsis, from the peak of their experienced perfection observed man living in society, and in their x-ray vision they could read how the mind and intellect of every individual react to the infinite variety of circumstances in life. In the four paths described above, the attempt is really to gain a greater control over the mind. Any practitioner in any one of the paths in the spiritual scheme will certainly come to have a greater mastery over his own mind, and the **mastery over the mind ends in a greater and intense integration of his personality. The more one gets integrated in the mind, the more dynamic becomes one's intellect.**

Thus purified, the mind and intellect equipment gains a greater efficiency and a greater power of flight. Making use of such a pair of wings, the individual soars higher into the brighter realms of spiritual perfection.

26. THE GOAL OF PERFECTION ACHIEVED

Religion is not for animals. It is essentially that which answers a special demand, which fully grown man alone makes in life. That there are no philosophies or religious ritualism in the world of the flora and fauna seems to be one of the wondrous and intelligent looking arguments of guided atheists, when they justify their reluctance in accepting religion. There are among men, those who have come up only to the animal level in their inner evolution. When in any generation the majority is of this type there will be a greater rejection of the higher values of life and the very quest of the Supreme would become unfashionable, almost insufferable.

The greater the integration within, the higher the individual's mind and intellect can fly, and the vision of the prospect below extends itself into greater distances when the observer is raised to greater altitudes. The greater the heights from which we look around, the wider is the prospect that unrolls under our gaze.

When integration has taken place sufficiently, the individual comes to recognize and feel a nauseating disgust at the mere life of acquiring and keeping, earning and hoarding, eating and wasting, sleeping and breeding, growing and dying, and he seeks and thirsts to discover in life, a greater mission and nobler purpose. He gains the capacity to look beyond the walls of his own house, beyond the streets of his own village, beyond the demarcation of his province, even beyond the frontiers of his own nation. He perceives in one dim look the entire life, as it is available among men, and he includes in his conception of life, the manifestation of it in the animal and vegetable kingdom of existence as well.

With this universal vision of the subtle mind, when the seeker in the fully grown man, comes to examine life as a whole, in his clarity of perception, he comes to see there, dynamic stages through which life makes its pilgrimage. At once, emerge out on the stage of life, endless number of beings throbbing with life; make an exit by the opposite side in their constant death! From the towers of the intellect, chastened and purified through any one of the processes of self-integration, when such an individual comes to recognize this phenomenon, he is embarrassed with a tragic and poignantly painful despair, almost amounting to a chaotic confusion.

At this stage of self-confusion, when he feels the problem to be too much beyond himself, he begins to make a closer study of his own earlier conclusions that:

"Life of man is arrow's flight,
   Out of darkness into light
   And out of darkness into light again;
   Perhaps to pleasure; perhaps to pain."
                                    — R.H.Stoddard

If life is thus a meaningless madness, in which we are all to sing a song of sorrow and slipping through stupidities, must end our pilgrimage from the womb to the tomb, then nature has gone off her nuts and she is to be considered a dangerous lunatic! It would be a wasteful extravagance on the part of the creator, if this entire scheme of the universe were a meaningless humdrum of chaos and confusion, of strife's and struggles, all taking us nowhere but to the cold embrace of the grave.

On the contrary, our Ṛsis of old, viewed life as one with the highest potentialities for perfection. If Darwin only visualized a greater and nobler stage of super-manhood, according to the Ṛsis, this super-manhood or godhood can be achieved by man in this very life through an intelligent process of self-integration and meditation. In their view, truth or the reality, is one and all-pervading in its absolute nature and therefore, they conclude that life must be the basis of everything perceivable in nature. Thus, they found that in all layers of life among the living beings and the existing things, life or truth expresses in varying degrees and in different languages. On the basis of this expression of life, the various equipment, constituted of the names and forms in the world were divided into four groups: (a) the inert stone-life; (b) the plant-life; (c) the animal-life; and (d) the man-life. In all these four layers of varying degrees of life, they tried to see the expressions of it.

Thus, they found that life in the inert stone just expresses itself, as existence, while, when we come to the plant life we see life has started expressing itself through their developed equipment in terms of a vague awareness of the outer world. Coming to the animal life, we find that they, compared with the plants, are enjoying a greater awareness of the happenings without perhaps to some extent, at least in some of them, a vague awareness of the happenings within.

But, in the finest equipment of man, we find the largest amount of 'awareness' or 'consciousness' expressed not only illuminating clearly and vividly, the world without, but with equal clarity the world within also.

Thus, when we view nature, we understand that beneath the superficial contentions of names and forms, the confusion of values and the complication of the problems of life, runs a scheme silently fulfilling itself. To complete this scheme, therefore, should be the grand aim of life. From the lowest evaluates, to the members of the highest grade developed, there is at every stage, a greater expression of consciousness and therefore to realize that in itself, if it is possible, would be the peaceful and perfect, the dynamic and divine goal of existence. In order that our mind and the intellect, body and its objects, may be driven to this self-discovery to be fully aware of the pure Conscious centre in ourselves, we have appeared in the field of activity with the sorrows of life. The limitations of power, the imperfections of the world, are all encouraging whips that make us run on the road, and reach our goal earlier.

The greater our identification with the matter envelopment, the greater our sorrows. To detach ourselves through right understanding and correct discrimination, from those with which we have no connection, is to reach ultimately the pure and the eternal Self in us. If a progressive liquidation of the perceived plurality, is thus possible as we view the pluralistic world from the deeper and subtler layers in ourselves, it appears clear, that there must be a still subtler fact in ourselves from the gates of which we shall have the vision of the all-pervading divine oneness in which love and charity are as natural as hatred and sorrow are ours today!

Life is one. A being is considered to be living when it is conscious of the outer world or both the outer and the inner world. Therefore, **to live consciously is to fully live the life, the life that is one without a second, everywhere, throbbing in and through the different equipment in different degrees of experiences.** The purer the mind and lesser the number of agitations, the greater is the consciousness that beams out through such an individual and he is a prophet, a saint, or a sage who gathers unto himself the world of beings in the compelling embrace of love.

Then he comes to experience and live entirely in unison with this sacred life as expressed through the multiple equipment, all round the universe in terms of Conscious Awareness. He is a Godman; his state is the Super-manhood. Such a man, call him Kṛṣṇa, or Christ, Mohammed or Mahādeva, Buddha or Śaṅkara, Vivekānanda or Dayānandā, Ramaṇa or Aurobindo, appears on earth to lead and guide his generation from time to time.

With the magic of his love, and the strength and sharpness of his wisdom, he tries to erase the animalism in man and to lift the entire generation to a higher pedestal of peaceful coexistence in a web of mutual love and understanding.

Rise and Fall of Man

If, as we said earlier, Consciousness or Awareness is our Real nature, and that evolution is completely fulfilled when we rediscover this state, then we must certainly seek the path by which we can regain this lost status of perfect Bliss. When one gets lost in a jungle, the surest, if not the easiest, path to return to the familiar grounds is to retrace one's steps. In order to go back to the pristine glory of our real nature, it will be easy for us if we investigate and discover the probable mistakes by which we have tumbled down into this dark well of sorrow and finitude.

We, from that state of transcendent glory, from that nature of Knowledge-bliss, have fallen to be men...limited, ignorant,sad mortals. How this seeming 'fall' has taken place is a necessary knowledge, so that we may know our path to return to our own home divine.

Vedānta does not accept any real 'fall' in man from the Reality. The Upaniṣads are never tired of repeating the assertion, '**Thou art That**'. Yet, you and I are feeling our separate existence, our weakness, our sorrows, and our limitations. It is always our bitter experience of the duality about us. The phenomenal world is evident, and minute to minute, it is experienced by us.

But Vedānta asserts that this seeming world of sense objects is not real. This is only a finite appearance. It can be ended. The world is seemingly real to us, just as the snake is real to the deluded, although there is really only a rope. The ghost is real to the frightened, who in his ignorance mistakes the post to be the ghost. Mirage can never be; even when we 'see' the mirage, desert alone is the reality in it!!

Thus, the eternal Sat-Cit-Ānanda alone is. The world and the egocentric ideas of our separate existence are only superimposition upon the Truth. They are all false. The plurality is a sad delusion. **The one alone is real and true.** Even so we are, today in our ignorance of the real, in our avidyā (nescience), living in our own delusions. How did this delusion rise up? This ought to be the natural question now in our minds. An attempt to explain this stumbling doubt in the minds of the seekers has been made in Vedānta by the introduction of the term māyā.

Māyā is defined as an inexplicable power of the Supreme, which is in 'That', as inseparable as heat from fire. Just as we cannot have fire, as a 'thing in itself', after removing all the heat from it, nor can heat have any existence if the fire element is removed from it, so too, māyā is a power inherent in the Supreme. Fire is heat, heat is fire.

It is possible that when we may have only a superficial understanding of this term, we entertain a growing suspicion that it is a tricky word introduced by the Vedāntīns in their Māyāvāda, to veil the main issues of a pointed question and to confuse the questioner with a mysterious nothing. But such a feeling can rise up only out of our own ignorance of the language; for in saṁskṛt, the word māyā in its etymological meaning, stands for, 'That which is not' (ya ma sa, maya) so that our doubts and suspicions need not have any play at all.

The famous story of the boy Somadatta's father in Vedānta is often quoted to explain the Māyā in us deluding us, as it were, with our own active cooperation and sympathy. Let us examine the story.

One newly initiated hermit, during a pilgrimage, felt tired and weary, one hot day in the burning sun. He, seeing a shaded arbour near the Ganges banks, took shelter there to rest. There was a narrow piece of rock upon which he stretched himself and composed to a restful siesta.

As he was dozing off, in those moments between waking and sleeping, his attention was attracted to two village girls who had come to the Ganges to collect water. They filled their pots and went away quietly. But the vision generated a line of thinking in the half sleepy hermit.

"Why not? Certainly there is no harm. Supposing I marry one of them. Then I shall keep a small little house; certainly there must be three spacious rooms at least. And I shall be a very severe and grave husband too."

"Working in my own fields. I shall live a happy life of contentment and joy. Then the first born...Yes, a fat, beautiful son. Of course, I must name him Somadatta. And we shall all three sleep in the same bed."

"But is there space enough for my son? Devī, please give some more space for our son; he might fall down."

"Lord, how can I" answers she, "Move? To where? You move a bit to your end."

"Alright" splash, ghu! G-h-u...o o o." Poor Somadatta's father moved a little towards his side and the stone was narrow. He lost his balance and rolled down into the Ganges waters. Awakened, the hermit swam out, and reached the shore.

Now, friends, what made the hermit fall? And after his awakening, where should he go to regain his young wife and only child?

The poor brahmacāri (hermit) created the world of Somadatta in himself, and identifying completely with it came to live the dream-life as though 'real' and thus suffered the fall.

So too, pure eternal Self we all are. The Self in a dream has forgotten itself, and dreams of its own saṁsāra. Wake up. Roll out of this narrow place and false identifications, dip into the cool Ganges waters...the Śrutis...and get awakened. End the undivine dream at one stroke!

The power in Somadatta's father, with which he lived his domestic life and ultimately fell down into the Ganges is māyā: 'that which is not' in his own mind existing as its own nature.

Māyā is manifested in the world as three distinct eternal qualities. The sattva(unactivity), the rajas (activity) and tamas (inactivity). All the three qualities are ever in a state of admixture. Their proportions of course vary from individual to individual and in the same individual it differs from time to time.

When the Supreme Reality, the eternal intelligence gets reflected in pure prominent māyā (guṇa pradhāna māyā) we get a very distinct and clear reflection of the Supreme in it; this is the God Principle. The reflection is dimmer in the sattva mixed with rajas and tamas (malina māyā). This is the egocentric jīva, individual mortal.

(Please refer to the chart attached at the end of this chapter).

The God Principle manifests itself around us in the world outside as three main accomplishments. We observe that at every moment, things are being created and born; at every moment things and beings are destroyed and dead, and certainly between these two points of an unknown beginning and an equally uncertain end, we also watch things and beings maintained. In order to facilitate the common man to grasp these three powers manifest about him, we have them represented as the Creator (Lord Brahmāji), the Maintainer (Lord Viṣṇu) and the Annihilator (Lord Śiva).

To create a pot, the potter must have pre-knowledge of what he is going to make; thus the creator ought to 'know' what he is to create. We have thus Lord Brahmāji married to Sarasvatī, the goddess of learning and knowledge. In order to maintain, we need the capacity to maintain. A pauper cannot be the head of the family and maintain the family. Thus, we have Mother Lakṣmī, the goddess of wealth and plenty as the consort of Lord Viṣṇu. Similarly, Lord Śiva cannot carry on the function of annihilation unless there be for him a field of finite destructible objects; without the phenomenal world, we cannot have the manifestation of the Rudra-might. So, Lord Śiva is ably supported by His devoted partner, Goddess Umā, the prakṛti.

Even when the Trinity is thus shown to be three distinct divine personalities, it is also shown clearly that they are distinct and separate powers divine. The oneness of them is the soulful song in our Purāṇas, but this subtle song is heard only by the most attentive and most cultured. In Sadguru Śrī Dattātreya, the teacher's teacher, we have a synthesis of all the three Lords, and in goddess Durgā, we have the representation of a total synthesis of the three divine consorts.

So then, whatever be the seeming plurality among our Gods, there is but one and the same God Principle. In fact, individually each of them is helpless; unless there is creation, the other two functions are impossible; without Viṣṇu the others are impotent; if Śiva-tattva does not function. Brahmāji or Viṣṇu cannot come to play at all. Only as a well organized team can the three together work and manifest. The one God Principle alone exists. The plurality is a delusion, a false understanding.

If the reflection of Truth in pure sattva-māyā is the God Principle; the broken, dim reflection of the same Truth Supreme in a medium of impure māyā is the individual ego centre, the saṁsārīn. The rajas is activity, the tamas is inactivity. This medium of reflection producing the jīva-dream is something like a cup of cowdung water reflecting the sun. The reflection cannot be as pure and steady, as clear and true to the original as the reflection of the same sun would be in a cup of pure crystal clear steady Ganges water.

How this dimness and agitations come to be, is represented on the right hand side of the chart appended at the end of this chapter.

The tamas quality acts in us in two distinct ways. It produces the mental agitation, vikṣepa and the veiling of Truth, āvaraṇa. Let us examine what these are: remember, these two powers are not fully independent; each depends upon the other. The vikṣepa creates the veiling and the āvaraṇa creates the agitations.

The veiling power of the tamas in us plays in us in three distinct negativities such as (a) Don't know (b) Can't understand, (c) Not experienced. These three negative concepts in us are removed by the three main items of the Vedānta practices: the listening (śravaṇa), the reflection (manana) and the meditation (nididhyāsana).

The first of three main tragedies, born of the veiling power in us, is that, left to ourselves, few of us have in us the capacity to independently observe, analyse and conclude that there is a God Principle behind the ever changing flux in the phenomenal world. 'I don't know' is the grossest state of āvaraṇa.

This is removed by listening, directly from the great masters, or indirectly through the great scriptures.

When we have removed this negativity, a subtler one rises up into prominence, viz. 'I can't understand'. This is surmounted by intellectual analysis and reasoning. When the seeker comes to feel that in and through the endless names and forms is running a golden chord of unity, a sense of oneness, the Ātman.

But often, students of philosophy at this stage learn to devalue their own intellectual awareness of this changeless Truth behind the medley of life, as not a practical fact, since it is 'not experienced' by them. This āvaraṇa manifestation in us is removed by the process of the practice prescribed for the Vedānta student called meditation. Meditation is a process of inner self-discipline by which through constant practice the seeker learns the art of keeping his mind at one and the same chosen line of thinking to the strict and severe exclusion of all other dissimilar currents of thoughts. Ultimately the sādhaka succeeds in bringing his mind to a complete stillness in which, unlike in sleep, he has his entire awareness brightly lit up and kindling in his bosom. At the moment of experiencing the transcendental Bliss and Knowledge, called Savikalpa Samādhi, the sādhaka comes to chop off his last traces of the āvaraṇa in his inner composition.

We have had so long a discussion of one of the manifestations of tamas-rajas impurities called mala. The other is the agitation of the mind called vikṣepa.

From this vikṣepa arises the unmanifest world, subconscious and from it spring forth the grosser emphasis and assertion of the manifest – the world of the five elements. The interplay of these elements produces the names and forms, including the senses of knowledge and the senses of action which together constitute the sad, tearful, ineffectual mortal, the helpless saṁsārīn.

With this, the fall of man (the arrow on the left side in the chart at the end of this chapter) is complete. From being the eternal, immortal, all-full (nitya, suddha, mukta, Paramātman), Pure Consciousness, due to the play of māyā, like Somadatta's father, we too have come to feel our own limitations and live in our unbuilt huts with our unmarried wife and unborn son, Somadatta.

Vedānta is not a pessimistic philosophy to leave its conclusions with a mere theory of fall. This very theory has been devised to explain the non-existent dream-fall so that the faithful may be shown a way to wake up and realize their own true and eternal nature, the Om.

All the different religions of the world and all the different yogas in Hinduism, however distinct they might seem to be in their approaches, in one voice insist that man must learn to control his organs of knowledge and action. Self-control without and within is the one point on which all religions sing in melodious agreement.

But, this control of the indriyas is not accomplished by a mere violent suppression. Deep in us lie the desires fed by our nescience. Unless this is ended by destroying the very source of it, the avidyā (ignorance), we cannot control effectively the sense organs. So long as traces of delusion are in us, we shall have desires rising up in us. They whip the indriyas to roam out among their respective sense objects. **With 'knowledge' alone can we end our 'ignorance'?**

The knowledge of our Real nature, the realization of the Śivo'ham state, the recognition that 'I am the eternal', the knowledge that 'I am not this'; name and form personality but one homogenous mass of Pure Consciousness, alone can end our ignorance (avidyā), the delusion (bhrāntī), the source of all the desire eruptions.

But Pure Knowledge is our eternal svarūpa, and so it is not a state that is to be created. We have only to end the clouding, confusing, deluding ignorance.

When the clouds move off, the sun, temporarily hidden behind, but ever lit and brilliant, reappears.

This removal of nescience is effected through listening, reflection and meditation, and we have seen how the veiling power of tamas acts upon us and how each of its strategies is met and defeated by the Vedānta practice of śravaṇa, manana and nididhyāsana (refer the chart).

Thus by the time the student reaches the manana-state, he gains more and more intellectual understanding about the futility of seeking some seeming happiness or any eluding peace in the world of sense objects. Here starts the real control of the sense organs. And when he gains slowly an amount of sense control, the agitation of the mind created by his contact with the world of sense objects get reduced. This enables him to gain a thousandfold more joy, peace and tranquillity within; and consequently his meditation-flights are higher, his intensity of concentration more pointed and firm.

Hand in hand the team works; the more the āvaraṇa is controlled, the more the vikṣepa is stilled; the more the tossing and agitations are pacified, the easier the veiling gets rolled off. In course of time, in proportion to the intensity of abhyāsa, the twin gruesome manifestations of tamas are both completely controlled; we shall then have sublimated the rajas-tamas defects (called the mala) in us with the consequent proportionate gain of sattva in us.

As we hear, reflect and meditate upon the Śruti mantras (the scriptures), the disturbances and the muddiness in our mental lake are eliminated. Naturally the pure sun of Knowledge, the eternal Truth gets reflected clearly. The clearest and the truest reflection of the Truth is the God Principle. Therefore, a sādhaka slowly comes to manifest in himself a certain amount of divinity and godliness at this stage.

Miracles are at this stage easy for him. Grace is natural. Kindness becomes his instinct. Love, his very breath. Mercy, his essence. Truthfulness his trait. Lordliness, his birthright. In short, a Godman on earth, he lives, poor or starving, suffering or in health, laughing or weeping, to rule, to guide and to enlighten.

At this stage, if he be yet steady in his sādhanā and can still maintain his divine urge to know and to become, if he has dispassion enough to reject and renounce even the powers and joys of godhood, he, during the highest flights of his deepest meditation, wafts even beyond the wonderful summit of sattva and becomes trans-sattva or sattvatīta one who has transcended even the guṇas. He experiences in himself the Truth Supreme, and becomes That. And having reached Om and merging there with Om, he becomes Om; he gains the Paramam Padam, the final goal of perfection, the Bliss Absolute.

There in Him rests all. The universe has risen only from Him; in Him it exists; towards Him it moves, into Him must it finally enter and ever afterwards becomes Him, the eternal Truth Absolute.

The arrow on your left (Picture 2) shows the direction of the fall of man from Om to delusion; and the consequent tears. The arrow mark on your right shows the ascent of man from the valley of tears to the state of Sat-Cit-Ānanda Self.

Thus, without control of the indriyas, without self-control, no spiritual growth is ever possible. And no control is effective until we start the listen-reflect-meditate schooling. Study the Upaniṣads. Independently think over them. Meditate regularly. Hand in hand, learn to control your senses. Through a control of desires intelligently pursue sādhanā. Success shall be yours 'here and now'; that is the guarantee repeatedly given by all the scriptures. With patience and faith **serve, love, purify, meditate and realise Truth** in this very birth.

"You can", is the confident assurance given by all masters to everyone who has approached them for guidance.

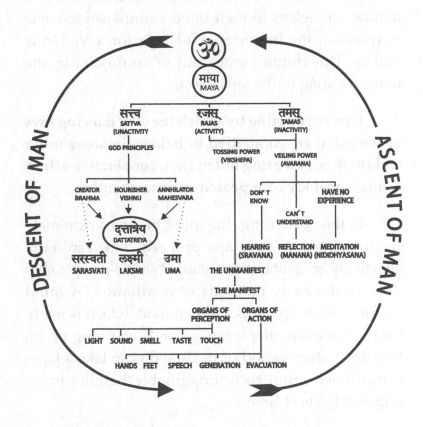

27. JAPA-YOGA

You may wonder why a student of Vedānta listening to, and reflecting upon discourses on the Upaniṣads or the Gītā should care to take up any method of sādhanā other than pure meditation. It is natural for seekers in their blind enthusiasm to come to question the importance of japa for a Vedāntic seeker. This doubt comes out of confusion in the understanding of the japa-yoga.

Japa is a training by which the ever dancing rays of the mind are compelled to behave in some order and rhythm, and bring out of their cooperative effort, a single melody of repeated mantra chanting.

In thus practising, the mind becomes extremely single-pointed. In fact, japa properly done can more effectively bring about a sustained single-pointedness than all the hasty methods of meditation. A mind seasoned with japa is like tinned food, which is ready for consumption after a few seconds warming up on the fire. A short period of meditation can take a japa-conditioned mind to unimaginable heights in an impossibly short time.

Japa is training for the mind in fixing itself to a single line of thinking. We cannot say a word without a thought-form rising up immediately in us; nor can we have a thought-form without its corresponding name. Try! Can you repeat the word 'pen' without its form? Can you? In this close connection between the name and the form lies the underlying principle in the technique of japa .

Again, love is not generated where sufficient thought is not bestowed. You love your near and dear relatives more than your uncle's sister-in-law's nephew, whom probably you had seen and even admired; yet, love is not there; for, you have not spent sufficient thought over that child. Thus, the japa in a prayer room performed in all intensity, and training oneself to repeat mentally His names constantly during the wakeful hours, are the sure ways of developing bhakti. It is always the repetition of thinking that brings about the fastness in all attachments. The less one thinks of a thing, the less one gets attached to it. The opposite is also equally true; the more one thinks of a thing, the more one gets attached to it.

The supreme Reality is experienced through meditation alone. But the boat to reach the goal, viz. meditation, is rigged with the practice of devotion through japa. In meditation one is wingless, if one has not acquired a decent share of concentration power and a perfect knowledge of how to fix one's mind at will at a single point for some length of time. Meditation is keeping the mind hitched on to one line of thought, to the complete exclusion of all other dissimilar thought-currents. To succeed in this we must learn to stop at will all other dissimilar thought currents. This mental capacity is gained through japa when intelligently practised along with a regulation of the normal life lived.

Japa is a very effective mental discipline for spiritual progress. In recent history there is the instance of the esteemed teacher of Śivājī, Śrī Rāmadās, who perfected himself through the japa-yoga of the Śrī Rām mantra: Śrī Rāma Jaya Rāma Jaya Jaya Rāma. Bhagavān Yogeśvara Kṛṣṇa Himself says in the Gītā : **"I am, among the yogas, the japa-yoga".**

"How must I start?" Do japa, is the way to perform the japa-yoga. What happened to the holidaymaker who waited on the seashore for the waves to subside so that he may take his bath comfortably? Don't waste your time in vain on the shores of life; get into the ocean of this Bliss and be refreshed.

Have a special room for your prayers; fix a charming picture of your heart's Lord, at such a height from the floor that when you sit in front of it, the Lord's feet shall be on level with your eyes. Spread a plain seat-āsana in front of your Iṣṭa; have a māla of 108 beads. Now start the japa, under closed doors please, to begin with. Sitting on the āsana in any comfortable legs-folded pose, in the beginning, gaze at the Lord's beaming face, body, legs, feet. Now slowly raise the gaze up from feet, legs and body, to the face of the Lord. Close the eyes now; feel His presence within you and try to visualize the Lord exactly as in the picture. This visualization of the Lord should be done within you in your love-heart, which is exactly on the right side of the physical heart. This is the spiritual heart centre where, if you meditate, your success is doubly assured. Feel...feel His presence.

Now repeat your Iṣṭa-mantra a few times, slowly, steadily, with all the love you are capable of. This prepares the bhakt in you to do japa most effectively. Take the māla; search for the off head; this is called the meru. Bring the tips of your ring finger and thumb together, and let the māla be hung at this junction. Repeat fervently your Iṣṭa-mantra; at each repetition turn one bead with the middle finger, always allowing the index finger to stand apart.

The index finger is considered to be an outcast because of its language. This finger is generally used in pointing out the 'other', in accusing another, in threatening, etc. essentially the index finger is used to express duality and the otherness of things and beings!!

When you have thus repeated 108 times your chosen mantra, naturally, you will come back to the meru-bead; you have now done one mālā. Now be careful: don't cross the meru; turn the mālā in such a way that the 109th mantra is counted on the bead with which the 108th mantra was registered. Thereafter proceed in all sincerity and finish your second mālā of japa. Thus do 20 mālās of japa twice a day – once in the morning and once in the evening.

A mantra is a word-symbol or symbols representing and expressing, as nearly as possible, the particular view of God and the universe they stand for. There is nothing secret about these mantras. All of them are in the scriptures, but when the mantra is given to the disciple by an illumined teacher, it becomes a living seed. The teacher, by his spiritual power, gives life to the word, and at the same time awakens the spiritual power latent in the disciple. That is the secret of the teacher's initiation.

These various forms of worship have been provided to suit the needs of different types of men at different stages of their spiritual evolution. This is just like a man, when he begins to learn writing. He draws first big scrawls, before he can successfully try a smaller hand. So too, a person must acquire the power of concentrating his thoughts by fixing the mind first upon forms, and then, after succeeding therein, by fixing it upon the formless.

Start today, right now. There is no moment more sacred or so auspicious as 'here and now' for spiritual practice. Japa is an easy method for men like us, kicked about and bullied by the worlds without and within.

(A) **Vedāntic Mantras** like:
Tat Tvam Asi – That Thou Art;
Aham Brahma Asmi – I am Brahman;
Ayam Ātma Brahma – This Self is Brahman;
Śivo'ham Śivo'ham – I am Śiva, auspiciousness;
Tadeva Satyam Tat Brahma – That alone is the Truth – That is Brahman;
Ānando'ham Ānando'ham – I am Ānanda, I am Bliss;
Haṁsā So'ham, So'ham Haṁsā – I am He, He is me, He is me, I am He.

(B) **Pauraṇic Mantras** like;
Om Namo Nārāyaṇāya
Om Śrī Rāma Jaya Rāma Jaya Jaya Rāma;
Om Namaḥ Śivāya;
Om Śrī Ṣanmukhāya Namaḥ
Om Śrī Rāmacandrāya Namaḥ
Om Śrī Lakṣmyai Namaḥ etc., etc.

can be taken up according to taste, faith and devotion for the purpose of regular, purposeful, intense chanting.

While doing japa, remember that even though the āsana, the beads-rolling, the Iṣṭa-devatā and such other equipments for japa are external, japa in itself is not physical but it is to be mental and is to be raised to a level very near to that of the spiritual. What I mean is neither a mere rolling of the beads nor a non-stop muttering in the mouth can constitute the japa-yoga.

It should be an all out intense and sincere effort of the japist to bring forth in his mind and intellect all the possible faculties like emotion, discrimination, sensitiveness, will, logic, reason, sympathy, love, faith and pour them all into the act of concentrating upon the 'mental chanting' of the sacred mantra, performed at the feet of the Lord's form, which is visualized steadily within the naked chamber of the bosom.

During japa, one's mind generally enchants the unwary practitioner into the jungles of unproductive thought-wanderings. If the student is not diligent enough to detect it and arrest the flow of thoughts, it is possible that his japa ends with his going into a dark ditch of impotency and stupor.

This warning is to be strictly given. Many of the japists, we see today in India, even all over the world in all creeds, have to a large extent, rendered themselves perverts. Strangely enough, we find that the ugliness of their psychological beauty is directly proportional to the amount of japa they have practised!!

To begin with, this seemingly simple yoga should not be over practised. Start with a mālā of japa a day. Slowly raise the number of mālās . You may start by increasing the number of mālās at first on convenient holidays only, and when you are convinced of your mental capacity to sustain your inspired attention for the required period of time, then alone should you take to long sittings at japa.

Another difficulty that comes to japist, and this is common to ninety percent of the japists, is an irresistible attack of sleep while doing japa and a shamelessly evident tendency to express bad temper soon after the japa-sādhanā. The seeker should not get annoyed at himself on these observations. He should learn to patiently fight these tendencies and win over them.

Sleep comes because a mind in japa is a mind at rest. Train the mind not to sleep in the salubrious climate within. It is natural for children to sleep in a running car and the poor things gain no thrill on the trip.

Bad temper comes because of two reasons – suppression of tendencies or fatigue. The former starts with the japist's own annoyance at his own mind wandering here and there during his japa . The latter is caused by exhaustion, because, to hold the mind in balance at a given line of thought is a great strain to the beginner and, therefore, his mind gets fatigued.

A new driver at the wheel knows not how to relax, and thus, exhaust himself before he has driven round the next corner of his own street; a new swimmer will be fatiguing himself within a few yards; a new housewife gets tired of looking after her very firstborn. Later on the very same woman easily manages her half a dozen, along with her late cousin's four little kids... and yet, discovers for herself plenty of spare time and mental ease for afternoon chat with neighbours.

There is an art of economizing energy in work. There is for every work, its own required stamina to be milked out from our individual personality. This is equally true in all spiritual activities called yogas. One's subtle judgement upon the works of an artist – as distinct from those of another – is not a detail, which is really taught, but it is that which, during practice, one comes to discover for oneself. The same rule applies in the art of yoga also. The artistic rhythm and harmony of any yoga will have to be discovered by the practitioner all for himself. This will come as a result of continuous practice in the right direction.

A japist's attempt is always to maintain his mind in one fixed line of divine thinking. To one who has gained a sufficient poise in this subjective art of single-pointedness gained through the practice of contemplation, to him, meditation is natural, for, meditation itself is but a conscious attempt to maintain the mind in one channel of thoughts belonging to the same species.*

Japa is thus a very healthy and effective aid to meditation, if properly practiced and regularly pursued.

Regularity and sincerity are the secrets of success in spirituality. Guard the mind against all excesses and make it immune to selfishness and passion. Watch how imperceptibly the mind ties itself down with things and beings, happenings and circumstances, by its own unintelligent attachments. Even when all these warnings are faithfully obeyed, there is still a subtle danger of the japa-activity being muddled with our incorrigible thirst for fruits. Profit motive is the strongest urge in man in all his strenuous activities. Japa , polluted by this profit motive (kāma), cannot end in the spiritual effulgence of the one doing it.

Consider the japa activity as yajña. Gather the purest and the best that you can eke out from yourself

---

* Refer for more details on Meditation to Swamiji's book entitled "Meditation and Life".

and offer them all into the japa as devoted oblations. The potential strength of blessing that lies dormant in japa will thereby be invoked, and to one who is under its grace, meditation is a homecoming, a pleasant and joyous ride through sunny fields and flowery gardens.

The effectiveness of japa to a large extent depends upon the spirit of surrender with which the seeker is practicing it. This idea of surrender should not be merely an emotional explosion of sentimental make-believe. It should be a solid act of understanding, at once deliberate and conscious. When once we understand the principle behind the surrender, we shall discover the bridge that connects the pasture land of bhakti and the snowy peaks of jñāna.

Let us for example take a typical mantra and try to discover the attitude of surrender implied in it: Om Namo Nārāyaṇāya—My prostration unto Nārāyaṇā'.

Prostration is not merely a physical act of bowing but it is a conscious act of discovering the greater in us and seeking our identity with it. To tune ourselves with the better or the nobler, and thereby gathering unto ourselves the very qualities and greatness of the higher, is true prostration.

In order to prostrate, there must be, at least, two factors; the lesser that prostrates, and the higher at whose feet the prostrations are laid. Within each one of us, there is the matter-conditioned ego and the unconditioned eternal Self. The japist in himself is trying to end his false ego at the altar of himself – The supremely divine Self, Śrī Nārāyaṇā. Thus, during the japa the individual practicing it will be sincerely striving to totally surrender his personality to Nārāyaṇā who is his concept of the Reality.

Thus, a mantra is but a formula that explains to us at once not only what is the enduring truth in life but also the technique by which we can reach it. Om is the symbol of the infinite, which is; finally, attained through surrender, (namaḥ) of all our false identifications with the matter-envelopment at the feet of **the core of things,** Nārāyaṇā. When our individual personality concept is removed from ourselves, we come to experience the Nārāyaṇā-tattva in ourselves which, being the same everywhere at all times is itself the expression of Om, the Brahman.

In fact, it is evident now, that japa properly undertaken is not only preparation for meditative flight but it can in itself serve as a vehicle which can lift us, from the pains and ugliness of our imperfections, to the very throne of the Infinite, the Perfect.

May you come to realise the joy and bliss of this Supreme Sādhanā – The Japa-yoga.

28. GĀYATRĪ MANTRA

Mantras are given out by the seers. Ṛṣis are the 'Seers' of the mantras meaning they are the men of wisdom who had realized the deep significance and the pregnant imports of the mantra. Every mantra has a presiding deity. The belief is that when one chants a mantra, one is to do so keeping in one's mind the form of the deity – then, like one being called by one's own name answers to it readily, so to here the devata is invoked easily. That is the faith. It is also the belief that on chanting any mantra ten thousand times alone can we hope to see any benign influence of the japa on ourselves. Whenever japa is undertaken, the form of the devata is to be maintained in front of the mind's eye. To facilitate this we have a meditation-stanza (dhyāna-śloka) that describes that devata, associated with every mantra.

Some insist upon the ritualistic formalities, prescribed in the upāsanā section of the Vedas, as unavoidable. the orthodox believe that, as the japa numbers mount up higher and higher, homa, tarpaṇa, large-scale feeding and such other sacred acts are to be performed as limbs of the japa-yoga. This view is not universally accepted as there is yet another powerful school who believe that sincerity and faith are the core of the japa-sādhanā, and anyone with a chaste heart of love can faithfully do one's japa , he needs no such formal and ritualistic entanglements to fulfil his sacred vow.

There are three types of mantras: those that invoke the low powers of nature (tāmasic), those that excite and manifest might and power (rājasic), and lastly, those that are of the quiet and purely spiritual types (sāttvic).

All those mantras can again fall under two classifications: (a) those that need to be only chanted, and there is no need for one to know their meaning; and (b) those mantras that are of the nature of an invocation, and the devotee must necessarily know the meaning of those mantras, without which he will not be able to bring his mind to play upon the divine theme constantly.

The Vedic mantras are both in poetry and in prose; the metrical mantras are called the 'Ṛk' and the prose mantras are called the 'Yajus'.

Of all the mantras the most powerful and the significant one is the single-syllable incantation called the Praṇava. This is the 'Om'.

The available literature upon the significance of this Vedic mantra is voluminous. Nowhere in the world can we meet with a more sacred symbol that has got such a vast amount of significance.

From Vedic times until the present day, the word 'Om' has been taken as a symbol and as an aid to meditation by spiritual aspirants. It is accepted both as one with Brahman and as the medium, the logos, connecting man and God. The entire history of the syllable is in the revelations of the Vedas and in the declarations of the Upaniṣads, and this history in the hands of the later philosophers developed into what came to be known as the sphotavāda or philosophy of the word. The perceptible universe is the form, behind which, stands the eternal inexpressible, the sphota, manifested as logos, or word. This eternal sphota, the essential material basis of all ideas or names, is the power through which God created the universe. Īśvara, the Brahman conditioned by māyā, first manifests Himself as the sphota, The inexpressible word, out of which He evolves as the concrete, sensible world.

There is a verse in the Vedas: 'Prajāpatir vai idam agra āsīt' (in the beginning was Prajāpati, the Brahman); 'Tasya vāk dvitīya āsīt' (next to Him was the word); 'Vāg vai Paramam Brahma' (and the word was verily the Supreme Brahman). The idea belongs to Hinduism and in the fourth Gospel of the New Testament we read it: "In the beginning was the word and the word was with God and the word was God." This sphota has its symbol in the word Om. Thus, in the Maitrāyaṇa Upaniṣad, after it has been said that there is one Brahman without words and a second, a word-Brahman, we are told that the word is the syllable Om. The sound of Om is also called praṇava, meaning that it is something that pervades life, or runs through praṇa or breath.

The very central theme of Māṇḍūkya Upaniṣad is the syllable Om through which the mystery of Brahman is gathered to a point. The text of this Upaniṣad first treats Om in terms of the Upaniṣadic doctrine of the three states of waking, dream and sleep, but then passes on to the fourth (turīya), thus transporting us beyond the typical Upaniṣadic sphere, into that of the later classic Advaita Vedānta. Speaking of Om, Taittrīya Upaniṣad says: "Thou art the sheath of Brahman". That is, Om is the container for the Supreme and, therefore, invoking Om is invoking the Supreme.

In every piece of music there are three aspects, viz. (1) the meaning of the song; (2) the laws of music and (3) the sound of the song. Similarly, in Om there are three aspects. The first is the mere sound, the mere mantras as pronounced by the mouth; the second is the meaning of the syllable, which is to be realized through feeling; and the third is the application of Om to our character, singing it in your acts and so through your life.

Om represents the Self, which is the Supreme non-dual Reality. The Self is known in four states, namely, the waking state, the dream state, the deep sleep state and the fourth state, called the 'Turīya'. All these states are represented in the three sounds of Om (i.e. A, U and M) and the silence that follows and surrounds the syllable.

The sound 'A' represents the waking state; the sound 'U' represents the dream state and the sound 'M' represents the deep sleep state. The waking state is superimposed on the 'A' sound because it is the first of the three states of Consciousness and so is the sound 'A', the very first of the letters of the alphabet – in all languages. The dream is but a view within the mind of the impressions that had reflected on the surface of the mental-lake during the waking state. Besides, the dream state occurs, between the waking and the deep sleep state and comes second among the three states of Consciousness. And so, 'U' being next to 'A' in order of sounds, and also as it is between 'A' and 'M', it is treated as representing the dream state. On the 'M' sound of Om is superimposed the deep sleep state. The comparison between the last sound of the Om and sleep is based on the fact that it is the closing sound of the syllable; just as deep sleep is the final stage of the mind in rest. A short pregnant silence is superimposed the idea of the fourth state known as turīya. This is the state of perfect Bliss when the individual self recognizes its identity with the Supreme.

In Om, the sounds A, U and M are called mātrās or forms; there is also in Om the common principle called the amātrā-Om which signifies the thing in itself, running though and pervading the threefold phenomena of waking, dreaming and deep sleep. The law of memory, is that the rememberer and the experiencer must be one and the same individual, or else memory is impossible. So, as we can remember all our experiences in all the three different planes, there must necessarily be a single common factor, which was a witness of all the happenings in all the three planes.* There must be some entity within ourselves who is present in the waking world, who moves and illumines the dream, who is a distant observer in the deep sleep world, and yet who is not conditioned by any of these three realms. This entity conceived as the fourth state, turīya, is the Real, the changeless, the Intelligent Principle.

The syllable Om symbolizes both the spheres: (a) the phenomenal, visible sphere of the 'Jagat', wherein the manifestations of time and space appear and perish, and (b) the transcendental, timeless sphere of the imperishable being, which is beyond yet one with it. Thus 'A', and the waking state, 'U', the dream state; 'M', the deep sleep state and the silence, turīya:

---

*Read 'Talks on Ātma Botha' by Swami Chinmayananda

all the four together comprise the totality of this manifestation of Ātman-Brahman as a syllable. Just as the sound 'M' manifests itself, grows, becomes transformed in its vocal quality and finally subsides into the silence that follows,* so do the four states, or components of being. They are transformations of the one experience, which taken together, constitute the totality of its modes, whether regarded from the microcosmic or from the macrocosmic point of view.

The A and U are as essential to the sound as M, or as the silence against which the sound appears. Moreover it would be a mistake to say that Om did not exist while silence reigned; for it would be still potentially present even in the silence. The actual manifestation of the syllable on the other hand, is fleeting and evanescent; whereas the silence abides. The silence, indeed, is present elsewhere during a local pronunciation of Om, that is to say (by analogy) transcendentally, during the creation, manifestation and dissolution of the universe.

It may be asked as to why this particular word Om should be chosen as the word representative of 'thought', out of which the universe has become manifested. The answer may be given in Swami Vivekānandā's own words:

---

* Which must be regarded as forming part of its sound in a latent, meaningful state of repose.

"This Om is the only possible symbol which covers the whole ground, and there is none other like it. The sphota is the material of all words, yet it is not any definite word in its fully formed state. That is to say, if all the particularities which distinguish one word from another be removed, then what remains will be the sphota . Therefore, this sphota is called the 'nāda-Brahman'– the sound-Brahman. Now, every word symbol intended to express the inexpressible sphota , will so particularize it that it will no longer be the sphota . That which particularizes it the least and at the same time most approximately expresses its nature, will be the truest symbol thereof; and this is the Om, and the Om only; because, these three letters A, U, M, pronounced in combination as Om, can alone be the generalized symbol of all possible sounds."

The letter 'A' is the least differentiate of all sounds. Again, all articulate sounds are produced in the space within the mouth ˆ– beginning with the root of the tongue and ending at the lips – the throat-sound is 'A' and 'M' is the last lip-sound; and 'U' exactly represents the rolling forward of the impulse which begins at the roots of the tongue, continuing till it ends in the lips.

If properly pronounced, this Om will represent in itself the whole phenomenon of sound production, and no other word can do this; and this, therefore, is the fittest symbol of the sphota , which is the real meaning of the Om. And as the symbol can never be separated from the thing signified, the Om and the sphota are one. And, as the sphota , being the finer side of the manifested universe, is nearer to God, and is indeed the first manifestation of divine wisdom; this Om is truly symbolic God.

'Om' thus represents the entire manifested world and the unmanifest, and also that which lies beyond both the manifest and the unmanifest – the Brahman, which is the changeless substratum for the changing objects of the world of experiences.

To every mantra, 'Om', the praṇava, is added on. Without 'Om' no sacred chant has its power. Just as a living body has no vitality when the life giving breath is not flowing through its veins, so too, a mantra has no life in it without the addition of the praṇava.

Vedāntic students generally practise the repetition of and the meditation on the symbol provided by the praṇava – this is called 'Praṇava Upāsanā'.

'OM' represents in its silent significance, both the manifest and the unmanifest, which together constitute the entire subtle and gross worlds. The word Loka in saṁskṛt is generally translated as 'world', but in its etymological meaning it signifies 'a field of experience'.

The entire possibility of experience in life has been terraced by the Ṛṣis into fourteen Lokas (world): seven higher Lokas and seven lower worlds. There are three worlds in which a limited egocentre comes to play its game of reincarnation and repeated deaths: these are (i) Bhur-loka, the physical earth; (ii) Bhuvar-loka, the world next to the physical and closely connected with it but constituted of finer matter; and (iii) Svarga-loka, the heavenly world.

Beyond these are the four other 'worlds' wherein the ego comes to move about and enjoy in its higher evolutionary life, and they are called the Mahar-loka, Jana-loka, Tapo-loka and Satya-loka.

In the Hindu literature, we also find conceptions of other worlds as: Indra-loka, Candra-loka, Surya-loka, Pitṛ-loka etc. which are special realms of experiences located within the above regions.

Below these seven worlds, there is yet another set of seven worlds called the 'Tālas'. They are named as Pātālam, Mahā-talam, Rasā-tālam, Tala-talam, Su-talam, Vi-talam and A-talam.

Of these fourteen 'worlds', Bhūr-Bhuvaḥ-Svaḥ, denoting the 'three worlds', are called the Vyāhṛtis. In the Gāyatrī mantra, when these Vyāhṛtis are chanted, the meditator can visualize the three worlds as arising from, existing in and disappearing into Om. He can subjectively identify them with the waking, dream and deep sleep conditions of the consciousness, transcending which extends the realm of the Infinite. All of them are represented in the symbol Om. In this sense the Vyāhṛtis in the Gāyatrī represent in one sweep the entire world of the subjective and the objective experiences of man.

The Gāyatrī Mantra
"Om Bhūḥ Bhuvaḥ Svaḥ
Om Tat Savitur Vareṇyam
Bhargo Devasya Dhīmahi
Dhiyo Yo Naḥ Pracodayāt"

The Hindu concept that the Gāyatrī mantra was declared at first by the creator Himself, at the very beginning of creation, may be considered as an over-exaggeration, which is an unavoidable feature in many portions of the Vedic literature. But it is also a fact that even the Western scholars, who have been accepted by all as having a better historical sense, have themselves declared the Gāyatrī mantra as one of the oldest available divine hymns. It is true that many revolutionary changes have taken place in our religious belief and yet, this mantra continues to persist and has even today a compelling charm of its own for millions of Hindu hearts. It is not only believed, but it has been actually observed that by the repetition of this mantra with the right understanding of its sacred meaning, the ordinary negative tendencies in a human mind can be erased to a large extent.

This mantra is never chanted for the purpose of material gains, physical or otherwise. Its very invocation concludes with an appeal to the Pure Consciousness to illumine our heart more, that is to say, it is a prayer unto the Self to unveil itself and come to manifest as pure wisdom in our life.

Gāyatrī mantra is otherwise called as Sāvitrī mantra. In the ancient Vedic literature this mantra was indicated familiarly as Sāvitrī and this term has been given to Gāyatrī because it is dedicated to the deity called Sāvitrī. In some rare old books, we find this mantra titled as Sāvitrī Gāyatrī; it only means that it is an invocation dedicated to Lord Sun couched in the Vedic-metre called Gāyatrī. This is considered to be the most important mantra, written out in this metre and, therefore, by tradition, this mantra has come to be known as Gāyatrī.

The Gāyatrī metre is generally constituted of three lines of eight syllables each. The three lines of Gāyatrī -Sāvitrī mantra are as follows:
"....................
Om Tat Savitur Vareṇyam

Bhargo Devasya Dhīmahi
Dhiyo Yo Naḥ Pracodayāt"

You will find in the above that the first line has only seven syllables. This is explained generally in two ways: (a) the syllable 'ṇiyam' is constituted of 'ṇi' plus 'am' and therefore, there are the required eight letters in the line, and (b) that the line is to be read along with Omkār which would supply the missing syllable. The former is the idea of Śrī Śaṅkara; in his commentary on Bṛhadāraṇyaka Upaniṣad, Śaṅkara splits the letter into its two components and considers that the rules of the metre are thereby fully obeyed. Gāyatrī mantra belongs to the Ṛgveda and it is found in the third maṇḍala, in its sixtieth sūtra as the tenth mantra.

The Seer of the mantra is that royal Saint Viśvāmitra. All the mantras belonging to the third maṇḍala of the Ṛgveda are attributed to Saint Viśvāmitra. The Gāyatrī mantra is also seen in the Śukla Yajurveda and Kṛṣṇa Yajurveda.

This mantra is dedicated to the Lord Savitṛ. That Savitṛ represents Lord Sun is the accepted version, even though there are some scholars who protest against this. The Sun gives all illumination to the world and any prayer for light should certainly be addressed to the source of all light in the material world, the Sun. In Gītā the Lord says, "The light that

pervades, the Sun and the Moon are all my Light".
Thus Savitṛ, the Lord of Gāyatrī, is nothing other than,
the light of Consciousness, the Infinite, the Absolute.

"………………….
Om Tat Savitur Vareṇyam
Bhargo Devasya Dhīmahi
Dhiyo Yo Naḥ Pracodāyat"

which means:

**"We meditate upon the auspicious godly light
of the Lord Sun; may that heavenly light illumine
our thought-flow in our intellect."** This mantra is
always chanted along with praṇava and the vyāhṛtis.

The usual prescribed daily worship (sandhyā
karma) of a Hindu, mainly includes repetition of this
Gāyatrī mantra. In the ancient days (sandhyā vandan)
the daily worship was only a purificatory act. It is only
a method of reintegrating one's own mind that has run
wild during the day and has drowned completely in
total inertia in the night.

In Manusmṛti we read: "In the early dawn by
doing this japa standing, one ends all sins committed
during the night, and by doing the japa in the evening
by sitting, one ends one's sins committed during the
day." Sin here means, as everywhere else in our sacred
books, the agitations created in our mental life by our
negative actions and the tendency to repeat the same,

which is left by them as impressions upon the mind.

It is only afterwards that the importance of Gāyatrī grew, to its present status. Later on, sometime during our steady slipping into our present decadent state, the belief that Gāyatrī cannot be chanted without the sacred thread became much rampant; a belief which we seldom meet with in the ancient lore. When we are thus daily using this mantra in our worship, it is chanted along with the praṇava and the vyāhṛtis. We may or may not add the praṇava to the second line:

"Om Bhūḥ Bhuvaḥ Svaḥ
Om Tat Savitur Vareṇyam
Bhargo Devasya Dhīmahi
Dhiyo Yo Naḥ Pracodayāt"

There are two sandhyās in a day. The term 'sandhyā' means the blending point of day and night. In the ancient literature we fail to find any importance for the midday worship. According to the Vedic literature, the Ṛṣis seem to insist only upon the morning and evening prayers. This midday prayer night have filtered into our creed, perhaps, as an unnecessary borrowing from the Mohammadan cult. Early morning, when the east blushes in light and in the evening when the golden light fades into darkness we have the two sandhyās . Generally, the morning prayers are done most profitably between 4.30 a.m and 5 a.m. which is called the Brahma-muhūrta; and in the evening the interval between 6 p.m. and 7 p.m.* is the sacred hour for the evening prayers.

"After getting up from bed, after answering the calls of nature, purifying yourself completely, disallowing the mind to wander hither and thither, sincerely perform the morning japa standing on your feet and repeating the mantra very slowly."

In Manusmṛti we find very interesting and clear directions on these prayers and worships.

"In the morning worship till the sun rises above the horizon, do the japa standing and in the evening worship, sitting down, do your japa until the stars emerge out."**

In the ancient days the daily worship (sandhyā karma) was not so elaborate as they have become now, after the days of the sūtras and āgamas. In the beginning the Veda advises us to sing the Gāyatrī mantra both at the dawn and at the dusk standing in water and facing the sun. Naturally, in the morning, the face will be eastward turned; and in the evening, the face will be westward turned. He who is chanting

---

* First show film-time of the modern man is the perfect sandhyā for the seekers of even our own times.

** Manusmṛti 2/101.

the mantra is to carry water in his folded palm and at the end of each mantra-japa he must offer that water to the Lord. This is called the offerings unto the great guest (arghya pradāna).

As this water in his folded palm is offered, the devotee says: "This Sun is Brahman" (Asāvādityo Brahma) and performs ātma-pradakṣiṇa; turning round himself by his right. This signifies a suggestion that the devotee is going round in reverence and devotion round the Lord Sun, the Brahman which is the Self in himself.

The Gāyatrī is chanted generally at each sandhyā, a minimum of ten times; but, however, according to one's faith, convenience and devotion one can chant any number of times as one likes in any sandhyā. But never is this mantra chanted at night; after the sunset Gāyatrī should not be repeated, is the rule.

In Taittirīya Āraṇyaka* we have in a story form a glorious explanation of daily chanting of Gāyatrī and the offering of arghya poured towards the sun. The story is a typical example of the Vedic style of mysticism. While describing the story, it is made to convey a deep significance in our subjective life itself.

---

* Āraṇyaka is the Upāsanā-kānda in the Vedas–the portion that connects the purely ritualistic section called the Brāhmaṇa with the essentially philosophic portion, called the Upaniṣads.

In an island called Aruṇam a tribe of devils called Mandehas live, and so their native island was also called as Man-deha Aruṇam. Every morning, these devils, in hordes, conquer space and reach almost near the sun threatening to destroy Him, which is when the water thrown out of the palms of Gāyatrī japists becomes lightning strong and the devils get struck by it and retreat back into their own island. This happens daily.

The story as such would read silly, but so too, the European music-page books for me! But when a man renders it eloquently upon his musical instruments, the silly page melts into a torrential downpour of harmony and rythym.

Mind (mana) and body (deha) are the sources of our activities* in the world outside and they, with their likes and dislikes, the emotions and appetites, their passions and cravings bring out from us a host of passionate animal instincts which try to conquer and destroy the spiritual essence, the Brahman, the Sun in us. The essential brilliance of the human intellect thus gets clouded by the approaching hosts of these passions and Gāyatrī japa and its consequent effects are thunder and lightning descending down upon them!!!

---

* Hence the name of the Island Mandeha!

Thousands of years after the Vedas, we have the Sūtras, whose authors recommended more and more items to be incorporated in daily worship. Following the Sūtras, after a time, the Āgamas came to be written and their authors had their own contributions to make to the general form of our daily worship. Āgamas mainly describe the ritualistic regulations and rules in worshipping Viṣṇu, Śiva and Śakti. Each Āgama claimed the Gāyatrī as its own; and they declare that Gāyatrī is presided over by Viṣṇu or Śiva or Śakti according to the name of the Lord that is recommended by Āgama.

The Śāktās gave the idea that Gāyatrī is the infinite goddess and made her a feminine deity; Gāyatrī Devī, who soon became the mother of the Vedas and even today it is very freely believed by brahmins that if they have chanted Gāyatrī they have chanted the Vedas.

Very many interesting but irrational, though quite effective, beliefs have arisen about the Gāyatrī mantra and its efficacy. For* any one frightened in the dark Gāyatrī mantra chanting is immediately advised to get over the nervousness of its fright. If anyone has some such delusory fright as a result of which the individual is prostrate with illness, then some Brahmin

---

* Personally I do not believe in these – but I am reporting here that those who are suffering from these mental weaknesses can find a consolation and true remedy by repeating Gāyatrī mantra.

priests of true devotion and pure moral life are engaged in conducting a congregational japa by the bedside of the patient.

These beliefs only prove that the very name of the mantra is fully justified. The term Gāyatrī itself means* "that mantra which protects him who chants it".

It is also believed in India that on starting any important great work, if a man detects some bad omen he must immediately sit down and chant the Gāyatrī eleven times. If on starting again, he meets with a new set of bad omens he used to sit down again and chant Gāyatrī sixteen times. This will remove the effects of the bad omen encountered, this is yet another belief.

In India, a Hindu boy is initiated into the Gāyatrī mantra very early in his life. This is done under the family social ritual called the Upanayana ceremony. In the Vedic literature we find mention of the Gāyatrī-dikṣā, the term dikṣā means a discipline which one must undergo in order that one may become fit for taking part in any Vedic ritual. The word Upanayana means 'bringing nearer', bringing near a preceptor who initiates the boy by giving him the sacred Gāyatrī mantra. It is interesting to note that there are definite prescriptions ordering the age at which the boys are to be initiated. Manu** gives the age as five for a

* Gāyantaṁ trāyate iti Gāyatrī
** Manusmṛti II: 37-38

brahmin, six for a kṣatriya and eight for a vaiśya; the maximum age at which initiation may be given are at the age of 16, 22 and 24 respectively.

The Vedic declarations glorify this saṁskāra-karma and insist that the life after the Gāyatrī-dikṣā is almost a second birth, since, in this ritualism, the boy is initiated into a new transformation in his subtle life. The father and mother have given birth to him from mutual desire and so he is born from the womb; let this be known as his physical birth. But that birth which is given, according to the ordinance, through the Sāvitrī, by the preceptor, who has mastered the Vedas, is the true birth, the unchanging and immortal.* After this initiation, the boy is considered as twice-born (dvija).

The full Gāyatrī mantra has got, in fact, a fourth line also** which invokes that which lies beyond the effulgence and it asserts in an intimate subjective experience of the devotee, his identity with it, as 'That is this'. The fourth line is referred to in Chāndogya, Bṛhadāraṇyaka and Brahma-sūtra. This line has been always preserved as very sacred and secret, and it is only given to full time seekers or to self dedicated sannyāsins. This line is not so much for chanting as for experiencing in the highest moments of intense meditation in samādhi.

---

* Manusmṛti II: 147-148
** 'Paro Rajase Savadom' – meaning 'he who is transcending the effulgence is this'. See Chāndogya 3:12:5; Bṛhadāraṇyaka 5:14:7.

In ancient days, ladies used to chant Gāyatrī as freely as men. So says Manu. In the ancient days ladies had their Upanayanam performed. They used to learn the Vedas, teach the Vedas to others and chant the Gāyatrī mantra. Here the term 'ladies' cannot, by any stretch of imagination, be conceived as meaning the ladies of the brahmin or the kṣatriya families only.

In fact, the spiritual unfoldment, through mantra upāsanā, is found more readily in ladies banning gentlemen, because the former has not the nerve-shattering personal contacts with the competitive problems of life. Thus the śāstra injunctions and our own personal observations take us to the conclusion that women too can, rather should, chant the Gāyatrī mantra regularly in their morning and evening worship.

In fact, there are repeated declaration in our Hindu sacred books that if the effects of the sādhanā performed by men are their own, the spiritual benefits acquired by the women folk are shared by the husbands, children, their families and the entire society.

The deeper philosophic imports of Gāyatrī are very clear.

The mantra, as it stands, obviously invokes the Lord Sun and pleads to him to illumine the intellect of the seeker. The sunlight cannot, it is certain, illumine in us the intellect... the white and grey matter of the brain!!

In our inner life the sun represents the light giver, the illuminator of all experiences, the Ātman. This Pure Consciousness in us, the inner centre of our personality, around which the matter envelopments function with mathematical precision... just as around the Sun, the entire solar system revolves each planet at its appointed speed and each along its appointed path... is being invoked to shine more and more in our intellect.

If the Sun were not there, life would have been impossible... without the Ātman the matter envelopment becomes inert and dead.

We appeal to this inner Sun of life to illumine the intellect. The infinite light of wisdom, the supreme Self is never contaminated in its eternal effulgence. It is ever the same. Its intensity cannot increase or decrease.

Therefore, all that devotee means is "May my intellect be steady without agitation; may it be clean without the dirt of passions, may the light of Consciousness come to shine forth a brilliant beam of its radiance through my intellect." Thus, may my perception of the world be clearer, my discrimination subtler, and my judgements correct and quick, my comprehension of situations and beings be precise and wise.

29. AT WAR WITH MIND

The technique of japa lies in engaging the mind totally in a self-repeated sound, having a very subtle and a great philosophical significance, and after a time when the mind is fully engrossed with the idea, we cry a halt to it, thereby taking away from the mind its only occupation at that time. The hope of the scriptures (Śāstras) is that by such a process the seeker would come to experience 'the silence of the heart'.

But, in fact, in our practice, we shall come to experience that, in spite of all the techniques and the underlying wisdom of it all, we still deceive ourselves, inasmuch as our mind still continues to wander. To gather this mind and to hold it as an integrated whole at the point of meditation calls for a painful and difficult strategy. This inner struggle is really the battle of Mahābhārata, and it is an eternal one. This struggle is the price that we must pay for the eternal reward of liberation.

Mind, we had seen, is a product of the impressions we have gathered so far in all our lives, from the beginningless time onwards to date. In all our incarnations, we have been living, moment to

187

moment, endless experiences and each such lived moment could not have but left a few dots and dashes on our mental sheath. Goaded by these impressions, an irresistible mind, wild and surging, drives our physical structure endlessly hither and thither. Tossed between them, we earn our agitations and feel shattered in our attempts at our meditations.

When the good and the bad meet face to face, there must be a field of tension and activity. It is an eternal law. We can never mentally get away from these two feelings, and as such, identifying with them we suffer the consequent dissipations.

At one moment we are identifying with the call of the good in us, 'the soft small voice of the within', and feel unhappy that, in spite of ourselves, we are tempted to act like the criminal, the vicious and the sinner. At another moment, strangely enough, in spite of our satanic inclinations, we succeed in doing good and feel elated. This tension between God and satan, the Pāṇḍavas and the Kauravas, within the bosom of a seeker is an eternal one. All the scriptures in the world unanimously declare that ultimately the success belongs to the Arjunas who have made the Lord of Vṛndāvan Himself as their charioteer.

To the seeker who has given up his body-chariot entirely to the supreme control of the divine charioteer, even disaster spells success! We will take up this analogy later in our discussions.

The challenge facing every meditator, as we said now, is the threat of the mind. The mind, by its very nature, is ever running into its own self chosen, instinct ploughed ruts. The seeker's attempt is to bundle up all the wasteful channels, and to make the waters of the mind run through a definite channel, and make it irrigate the field of the divine, within himself. A thorough knowledge of the strategies of the mind and a full control of ourselves, by which we can hold the mind back to the point of concentration becomes absolutely essential, if we are to win ultimately in this subjective war against our own lower self.

The following methods may be employed with success. Not all of them at once, but anyone of them would be sufficient at any given time. If you discover that you have used the wrong missile, you can always change the instrument and win your moment-to-moment victories. I am giving you here a long list of the weapons available in the arsenal of the scriptural seeker. Almost all of these have served me faithfully on many occasions.

(1) Whenever the mind runs, to become aware of it and at once strive to bring it back to the point of meditation forcefully is one of the methods. This is in fact, the goal and the means, both in one. Gītā and other sacred books (Smṛti and Śruti), insist upon this.

(2)   We often find that a wandering mind is a mind, that has gone forever from its aim of concentration (lakṣya) and we too, invariably go with the mind and do not recognize for a long time that our mind is wandering. Therefore, the remedy should lie in ourselves. When we are sitting for prayer and meditation we must be fully conscious of what we are about. It is for this purpose that we have congregational prayers, chiming of the bells, incense burning, beautiful lights and Lord's form or symbol. Every religion insists that before prayer we must physically cleanse ourselves and wear clean clothes.

If the temple of God is in no way different from a third class railway waiting room, we shall have as much peace and concentration in the temple as we have in the railway station. Unfortunately, of the religionists in this world, the Hindus, in this respect, are the dirtiest of the lot! They are ignorant, careless, indolent and stupid. Rarely indeed are our temples clean, not because there are no hands working incessantly to keep them clean but, the rate at which the devotees dirty it is faster than the rate at which a few hands could clean it off.

It is a truth that in a dirty room, in dirty clothes, under dirty wrappers, we cannot meditate properly. **Cleanliness is next to godliness.**

(3) In a clean room, or in a clean corner of a room, after ablutions, when we sit on a clean seat, in front of a symbol of the Lord, sufficiently captivating to the mind, and indeed fully entertaining for the intellect, we can have all the necessary protection against the mind's wanderings. Making use of these, when we try to meditate, there are again the subtle causes rising from the inner world, which also try to sabotage our efforts. Our love and hatred, hopes and demands, desires and passions, make the inner world dirty, and propelled by them our minds fly at a tangent in their roaming. These wanderings are held back by singing the Lord's glories with eyes open.

Here too, we can deceive ourselves; and more than 99 percent of the religionists all over the world are doing it today. They make a great show of their devotion and scriptural learning, of their rituals and the paraphernalia attached to their religion, all a mere crude superficial show. Such devotees are suffering from exhibitionism rather than blessed by any true spiritual urge; they are not seekers, but suckers. **It is clear then that sincerity of purpose is the secret of success in spiritual seeking.**

(4) Our religion liberally provides us with a sufficient field for practice in meditation.

Generally, an uncontrolled and raw mind wanders into limitless fields; now in heaven, now in hell, now here with us, now here with everybody. All of a sudden to control such a mind would amount to a degree of suppression, which is not healthy. Thus, in all religions of the world, we are given authorized versions of the history of the Gurus or the achievements of some Godman upon earth. To read such stories and to meditate upon the Lord's divine play on the stage of life would be to give our mind a large field, and yet a field that has an integrating principle underlying its every detail, namely, the Lord Himself.

Reducing even this field to one single incident in Lord's life, which perhaps attracts you the most, and to meditate upon it would be training the mind to restrain its activities to a more limited area. From this stage, to fix our attention upon the Lord's form only (or upon a symbol such as the cross or the crescent, or the book) would be still further reducing the area of our attention. Even here, there is certainly a conspicuous field for the mind to wander among its pluralities; the Lord's feet is not similar to His hip, the hips are certainly different in shape and suggestion from the divine chest, and the sacred face is still different from the limbs or the trunk.

Again, to aim still nearer to the bull's eye, almost its innermost circle would be when the mind comes to meditate upon merely the face of the Lord. Eliminating all the different details in His face, to make the mind steadily concentrate upon His divine lips and blissful smile of joyous perfection, is to reach a very high point of concentration through the pleasant path of devotion. When a seeker has reached this stage and when he can easily maintain himself in this field of intense concentration, he is almost at the doors of Truth.

The smile of the Lord is now the point of concentration, but, even here, there is a suggestion of plurality: There are the two lips of the Lord; the upper is different from the lower!! And again, there is a sense of plurality between the lips and their smile! With an effort, which would be the last and the final, the seeker is then advised to negate the lips and meditate upon the smile. Anybody who is trying this would then realise that to meditate upon the smile is to live in the smile and its voiceless message, in the Lord Himself!

In all this the devotee depends entirely upon his devotion or love for the Lord, and his success at concentration or victory over his mind, is entirely dependent on the amount of love he can bring to bear in his all-surrounding devotion.

(5)   During the practices (abhyāsa), the seeker must
       consider his mind with an attitude of motherly
       botheration, full of love-prompted anxieties.
       Watch how a loving mother intelligently tries to
       control her child in its mischief! Those tactics are
       all available for the seeker in controlling his mind.
       Persuasion is one of the most common methods
       of all mothers. To persuade the mind, to realize
       the glories of meditation as its highest vocation
       should be a daily preoccupation with all seekers.
       The more a seeker is convinced of the profits that
       he would gain by his activity in his prayer-room
       (Puja-room), the more shall he find that his mind
       is peacefully settling down to meditation.

(6)   Sometimes, a mother would persuade the child
       by offering it something quite tangible by which
       to win its attention and take it away from the
       particular field of mischief in which it is found
       to be indulging at any given moment. Thus, a
       mother would say to the child playing in the Sun,
       "Come here, baby, I shall give you something. I
       have been keeping it for you for the last two days,
       but I somehow or other, forgot all about it. You
       come here; I shall give it to you". The child
       hearing this starts wondering what this thing
       could be, and his curiosity pleads to him to
       renounce the playfield and to run to his mother,
       if only for a few moments, to satisfy his rising
       curiosity.

Similarly, the mind also, when it is wandering in its usual fields of sensuousness, can be pleaded to come back by repeating to yourself the blissful experiences of the great masters, their promises and their perfection, which they had acquired through the process of meditation. The curiosity of the mind is kindled and for its satisfaction at least, it would for the time being, come back to apply itself to meditation.

(7)   There are moments when this also fails, but the inexhaustible armour in the mother's loving heart has many more secret weapons to fight against the dangerous tendencies of the child to do mischief. For example, the mother would promise the child a greater freedom for a much more appetizing mischief, at another period of time.

For example, she would say, "If you would now come baby, and sleep in the afternoon, I shall in the evening, send you to the children's park, where you can play till nightfall on the swing and the seesaw!" The child for a moment weighs the pros and cons of the proposition and invariably it comes to understand that after all it is very profitable to renounce the game in the hot sun for sometime, so that later on it can play in an ampler field with greater freedom and surely with a much higher return in pleasure.

Similarly, during meditation, when the mind wanders away to worry over the domestic or the official problems, to worry over the market place or the international situations, to worry over its own weakness and of others, near and dear to us, a true seeker, diligently practising, can persuade the mind to come back to meditation by promising it a free ride into these fields of thought, say 'after lunch'. This concession may be given on a condition, strict and severe, "If you now totally reject it and cooperate entirely with me in my meditation". Without fail, you will experience that the mind, after a moment's hesitation, becomes supple and comes back to play the tune that we want it to play.

(8)   There are moments when, even the best of mothers know when the child needs a little bit of the cane-treatment. At such moments, and it certainly must be very rare, the mother not only threatens the child, but executes the threat strictly upon the child. In sheer fright, it quickly gets over those extremely wrong tendencies in behaviour.

Similarly, we must also, now and then, severely reprimand the mind and execute faithfully the threats held out to it for all its serious crimes. The only whip that can directly reach the mind is starving or fasting. When you detect that the mind is uncontrollable and is behaving most bull-like, lusty and sensuous, persuade it to behave properly but in spite of that if it be wild, show it the rod, and punish it with a complete fast for the following 24 hours.

In winter days, you can punish the mind indeed very severely, if you prescribe for the body a real cold shower bath! But here be careful; pneumonia is no respecter of personalities or their spiritual aspirations!!

We should not overdo it. A healthy mind can be had only in a healthy body. If the body gets too weak, the mind will become more and more fatigued and a fatigued mind cannot live in severe self-discipline. In these cases, each must become a judge unto himself. Again, another thing to be noticed very carefully in this strategy is to avoid becoming too lenient with the mind after having passed a judgement of condemnation. It may be possible that you may detect the mind at a crime and might in your sense of judgement give it the maximum punishment, which it so deserves. And yet, you may get into a wise after the event mood and may cool down to sympathize with your own mind.

Thus, having punished the mind with a 24-hour fast, you may become so lenient as to stuff yourself with fruits and milk thereby almost over feeding the body and the mind. Mind is made up of the subtle aspect of the food, which we consume, and so, denial of food, is almost denial of its own nourishment to the mind. But instead of the ordinary food, if the mind gets as a punishment, better food of fruit and milk, we shall find the mind repeating the same act as a result of which it has come to this great fortune! If the conditions of the slum areas are so bad that in comparison the slum dweller finds that jails are palaces, we shall find the criminals striving to go back to the jail as soon as they are out!

If you doubt what I say, go to any magistrate's court in our country and meet the delinquents or the criminals and have a very intimate and personal chat with them. Eighty percent of those who today are in the Indian jails, I remember to have read very recently, are all 'old birds' flown back into their own sequestered and comfortable 'homes'!

Once having taken the decision to punish the mind, the seeker should not, on any score, become sentimental and yield to the temptations to eat again.

No intelligent mother would over-punish the child, for; experience proves that over-punishment is as detrimental as over indulgence to the child's independent growth of individuality. Over-punishing the mind will make the mind, though controlled, ineffectual and impotent and such a dead mind is useless for higher meditation. The most effective punishment for the mind is for you to remain in yourself as though apart from the mind, watching with a critical eye its meaningless somersaults.

When a mother finds that her child is uncontrollable and, in spite of all the previous tactics, the child is still indulging in mischief, she comes to the verandah of the house, and leaning on to the pillar, stands merely watching the child at mischief with a pathetic look conveying to the child her sorrow and despair. The child steals a few glances at the mother and reading her sorrow, comes to its sense. It feels ashamed of itself and quietly retires, and from behind, it would hold on to the sari of the mother under some pretext or the other, demanding of the mother some special attention! At this moment, no intelligent mother will start scolding him, but will quietly take everything for granted and attend to the child's wishes, which are in fact, nothing different from the mother's own demands!

(9) Similarly, when the mind is uncontrollably agitated and runs about wildly, we can, identifying ourselves with our intellect, watch in perfect detachment the mind in a spirit of sympathetic criticism! The mind may still wander for sometime in its own self-appointed fields of activity, but it realizes that it is directly under the observation of an uninterested intellect, critically and continuously observing it from the towers of discrimination, and it becomes, as it

were, self-conscious and ashamed of itself and retires from its questionable vocations and nestles itself at the feet of the intellect. You will find then that the mind is available and ready for application at meditation. This technique is called, in our Śāstras, as the technique of 'witnessing mind' (sākṣi-bhāva).

Any one of the above methods should answer your problems at a given moment. A diligent practitioner can certainly discover for himself new methods and ideas to circumvent all novel mischief of the mind. In all these, the most important factor is that we must have a deep sense of sincerity, a great conviction born of faith and understanding and a hardy sense of seeking, at once adventurous and revolutionary. Without these great and noble qualities of head and heart, nothing can be expected out of spiritualism.

To wait for these qualities to descend upon you from the heavens or to hope to earn them by pickpocketing a Guru (teacher), is like waiting for somebody who has not been born to come and feed you. Strive hard. Act diligently. Meditate regularly. Discriminate continuously. Be good. Do good. Be kind. Be tolerant, merciful and all loving. Eradicate weaknesses steadily. Grow in your own inner strength. Keep brahmacarya, good company and good health. Even when threatened with death, renounce dishonesty, deception, lust and passions. And then meditate.

"Meditate, meditate, meditate and meditate. This is the only path, the only true path to Perfection; quick, easy, simple."

30. THE SECRET OF ACTION

(Talks delivered by Parama Pujya Swamiji to the Staff of the Central Secretariat, Government of India).

THE INEVITABILITY OF ACTION (Talk I)

Nowadays, under the modern system of education, when a young man comes out of the University, there seems to be this misconception in him that higher the standard of living, the less should a man work in the world outside. Thus mathematically, higher the standard of living, according to this misconceived notion, the less the work, and ultimately what would be the highest standard of living? No work at all. So, no work, maximum recreation, all sensual enjoyment, living 365 days in holidays! This is the highest standard of living! This seems to be the conception of our youngsters today when they enter into the field of action.

There seems to be, an unhealthy competition today among the workers. I have been mixing with the secretariat workers all over the country and I have noted that among themselves there is almost a competition like this: "How much did you work today?" "Three letters!" "Three letters you did! I did only one letter." Thus, the former decides that if the later had done one letter, "Dekho (see), tomorrow I will not do even one". Thus, there is a competition in the wrong direction today, because of this false notion, "I give my proprietor the minimum, and eke out of him the maximum".

This is nothing but a reaction.

When the foreigner was in the country under the medieval economic set-up of this country, the kings, the landlords and the proprietors, a few in numbers, learnt the art of squeezing the maximum out of ordinary people and arrogated all to themselves. Now, therefore, we find this reaction in the society that the average man or middle class man wants to get everything from the rich or the government without returning anything to the government or to the proprietor. This is a natural social incident, which happens inevitably in the context of our history, emerging from slavery to freedom.

But in this context, at this moment, when our nation's progress is at stake, if the young men who have come now, who are no more the children of the slaves but who are the proprietors of a new chance given to them by history, want to make their life and their country progressive, there must be a new philosophy of action in their hearts. Thus, after so many years of freedom, slowly the government and the industrialists have started realizing this, and great men, specialists from America have come to the country, and they give to the people in the country, the workers as well as the clerical staff, the ideas of the sanctity of work, etc., as if it is not in our culture or in our scriptures. It is already there but the 'Pundit-class' (educated class) was not bringing it out in the context of an independent country, panting to build up its destiny.

When we look at life, it is clear that if action is stopped, the organism is dead. Think for a moment please! You are all alive, I am also alive. The world belongs to the living. To the dead, there is neither a constitution nor progress nor industrialization nor is wealth nor happiness, there is nothing. The destiny of a nation belongs to the living generation. We are all alive. What do we mean by "we are alive?" Life is the most sacred wealth that you and I have got, we are ready to do anything to maintain that life; we worked or we studied in our childhood, we struggled hard for a job and we got the job, we are working from morning till evening now, all for maintaining our lives. Life is a common denominator. There is no question of 'haves' and 'have-nots' as far as life is concerned. Life is for the rich, life is for the poor, and life is for the employer and for the employees. Life is for the successful and for the failure. Everyone has got life and has equal share, and this we sacredly guard for ourselves. This is our precious wealth. But **what exactly is life?** Very rarely we are instructed in this either by our parents or by our elders or by our university education. We are very rarely given to thinking about it.

The great Ācāryas of the past also contemplated about it and they discussed this matter with their disciples. What exactly is life, then?

Life is a fascinating power, which expresses itself through the mighty man as well as the scoundrel. This expression is common to all of us.

What exactly is life? The teacher of the Upaniṣads, instead of defining life, asked the disciples to watch and observe a dead body. We call it dead, when all the activities in it have ended. The dead body is no more physically perceiving anything, mentally cannot have any impression or feelings, intellectually it cannot think. All its organs have stopped, the heart is no more thudding, and the physical structure is no more functioning within. At that time, we say that the organism is dead. Whether it is a human being, an animal or a plant, an organism is dead when it no more responds to the world outside.

There is a plant, I water it regularly, but still not a leaf or flower comes out on it. Then, the plant must be dead. Why? Because, it is not responding to the external stimuli. If a dog is lying down, and I throw stones at it, and yet it is neither getting up not barking, then we say it is a dead dog. Why? It is not responding to the pain caused by me. I call my father, I hug him, I love him, but he is not responding to any emotions of the other world. Naturally, we say the individual is dead. Whether an individual or a single unicellular organism, if in none of them there is any activity, then the organism is dead. **Activity is the insignia of life.**

You and I, when we are living cannot but be active. So long as we are living, we will have to act, for, life pulsating through the body is activity in the outer world. There is a fool, an idler; we ask him, "what are you doing my boy?" He says, 'nothing'. When he says 'nothing', the answer does not mean, that he is dead, but it means that he is not doing anything good with his activity either for the society or for his family or for himself, because action must necessarily come out of him just as fragrance from the rose. The rose cannot stop its fragrance from spreading out. If it is a rose, it must have the fragrance of the rose. If it is water, there must be fluidity in it. It is its characteristic, it is its nature. Similarly, you and I, until we are placed in our burial ground, will have to act whether we like it or not.

Now the question is: since actions are flowing out from every living man until he dies, how can they be organized, altered or disciplined in order that these actions, necessarily and inevitably coming out of him, would bring about happiness all around in the community and a sense of fulfilment and satisfaction to himself in his own bosom? This is what is called **"The art of action"**.

Action is inevitable, because it is the signature of life. Life expresses itself in action, as death does in inaction. But actions may vary, as they do vary, from man to man.

A labourer, working in the field may be perspiring and sweating. A poet, working may not be perspiring or sweating; he is seemingly, from the labourer's standpoint, not working at all 'From the standpoint of the poet, the scientist is wasting public money. From the scientist's standpoint an ordinary thinker is wasting his time. From all their points of view, the Buddha under the tree is a waster and leech upon the society, sucking the blood or the wealth of the society, an idler, etc. Each one may point out to the other and say that he is an idler, but each one knows how vigorously he himself is active.

It is said, that a great painter was once upon a time sitting down near a wayside pool and throwing stones into the water and watching the play of the light and shade upon the ripples. An ordinary man, moving along the road, carrying the milk from his cow-shed to the nearby town to sell the milk, jealously looked at this man and said: "This fool is sitting idle from morning till evening. What a dirty fellow! I have already put in eight hours of work, and I cannot make both ends meet." He murmured like this and went to the town. There, he sold the milk and as he returned with an empty can on his shoulders, he counted the money. He said "this much for the cows, this much for the fodder and this much for the family". And he sighed that there was nothing of a reserve to keep for his old age. He was disgusted with life and at that time, lo! Do you know what he saw? The same fellow was sitting in the same pose, continuing his stone throwing on the same pond, with one hand biting a pair of sandwiches. The poor milkman stood there and he could no more control himself and just like any of our local socialist or communist followers he stood there, and few more persons joined him – and started howling, "If there is a government in this country, such a rascal as this must be shot dead, because he has not been doing anything at all and I do not know what is the system of economics in this country that such an idler in the society has got the sandwiches, while I have not eaten at all from morning till evening. I have been working and I have not got anything for me to eat. What an injustice!" Poor villager, he knew not that the person against whom he had complained, was no less a person than Medici, the great painter, who as a result of observing those waves, reproduced them on the canvas, and there even today we can see the immortal picture of Madonna and the child, the Mother Mary with the Christ, sitting near a water pool, a lotus therein slightly moving in the breeze. He wanted to capture the play of light and shade on the waves, so that he could arrest them and capture them into the canvas, and he was most vigorously working in his own way but the others thought, that he was idling away his time. It is that man, the so-called idler who produced the immortal picture of Madonna and the child, while the milkman who is supposed to have worked and toiled so honestly for the society, died like a bug in any third class compartment of the Indian Railways! He died, leaving nothing for posterity to remember him by.

Everybody must work, but what matters is how to work, in what way one should work! Being in the sun for the whole day alone, is not work. That is one method of working. Another man may be in the air conditioned room for 12 hours but he too works, in his own way. But what is the type of work that we do? What type of work can we do and how the maximum can be brought out from ourselves? We will go into them in the following talks.

So long as we are living we cannot but act. When we are looking at it from the historical point of view, we find the old barbarian going about with a stone in his hand to destroy animals to eat them for his own belly's sake, thus he was working. The people of the Middle Ages were also working. Today in this age of the atom bomb and the hydrogen bomb, we too, are working. This work, we find at the same time, is not of the same calibre but differs from individual to individual.

The great Ṛṣis said that the type and the quality of work that we pour out of ourselves could be classified under three different categories. The first of them, they said, is the lowest type, and since I do not have a proper word in English, let us call it as 'labour'. When I say labour, I am not in any way bringing disgrace to the ordinary labour. It is not in that sense of the word that I am talking. By labour, I do not mean wearing shorts and banian, and working with the spanner and the screwdriver in hand. It is not that labour that I am talking about. Give me time enough to explain.

Ask a labourer, "Why are you working?" Then you will understand what is the quality of that particular man's activity. If you ask a man who is working, "why are you working" and the man answers, "I am working so that I may get my wages". The man, who is thus working in society only for the sake of wages, only for the sake of pay, only for the sake of commission, the man who is working in the world only for profit, is called a labourer. A minister may be a labourer, a Chief Justice may be a labourer, one of the greatest men of a country or a politician, may be a labourer, if he is putting forth his intelligence, mind and body to the society only with the idea "I will aggrandize more and more income". You ask him, "Why do you want wages?" He has no greater motive than "I may feather my house beautifully, for the sake of my wife and children; I want this income so that I may keep the wolf away from the doors; I want it only for my own pleasure." The man who is self-centred is working only for the profit that comes to him; with that profit he is not thinking of starting a hospital or doing any good to the society but he wants only to aggrandize and give it intact to his wife and children at home. If that is the low ambition with which a man is pouring out his energy in the world outside, the sweating man falls under the classification of 'labourer'.

In the same work that a labourer is doing and in the same field, there can be another man who is not a labourer at all. In a field where a great man of the stature of Mahatma Gandhi is gaining the greatest achievement, in the same political field there can be a man who is only a labourer. I hope I have conveyed the idea. It is not the work that you do that matters. It may be a scavenging work; it may be the Chief Minister's or Prime Minister's job. It is not the work that gives you the dignity and glory in the society but it is how you do it, and if you are doing it with an idea, "I may get out of society something and with that I shall benefit myself and enjoy myself in society". If this is the self-centred limited point of view, you may be a scientist, you may be a great thinker, you may be a poet, you may be a writer, you may be intellectually the greatest genius of the country, and yet you are only a labourer from the philosophical standpoint.

The second variety in contrast to the labourer is called the 'worker'. You will wonder, labourer and worker, where is the difference after all? I will bring home to you the difference. "There goes a political worker" we generally hear. But have you ever heard, a political labourer is going. Have you ever heard, religious labourer is going; a social labourer is going; social labour welfare? You do not hear so. 'Social labourer', we do not hear. "What are you doing?" Nowadays "I am doing social labour!" 'Social labour', we do not say. We say, "I am a social worker, I am a political worker, I am a religious worker, and so on". Then why do we say 'worker' as a contrast to 'labourer'? There is a certain difference.

To a worker if you ask: "Oh, political worker, why are you sweating like this?" He will say "that is because I want to bring about something in the society." "What is it that you want to bring about?" He will not say, "I will get so much profit." His eyes are not on the profit. No doubt, he wants profit. Besides that he wants some success in the society.

If you ask a worker why he is working, he will say: "I want success; therefore I am working hard". The labourer is asked, "Why are you labouring?" He says 'wages'. The worker wants success. "Success in what?" Every worker has a picture of an ideal heaven, of a perfect society; the idea may be a socialistic pattern or a communistic pattern or a divine pattern. But he has got a picture of an ideal and he is invariably struggling hard to bring about that ideal, as an actual fact around him, in his own lifetime, if possible. The socialist wants the socialistic pattern in society before he dies. The communist wants to bring the communistic pattern. Thus, each one has an ideal in his mind, and he struggles to make the ideal an actual fact. Such men are called 'workers'.

The worker is working not for mere profit, nor for the wages; what he wants is an idealistic pattern, which he has in his intellect, which he wants to bring about and work out in society. To the extent, the ideal is worked out in society, to that extent he is happy and he says, "I have succeeded".

Thus, a labourer wants wages, so that he may be happy with his wife and children. A worker wants success for the ideal he has. He wants to bring it out in society.

The third are the rare ones. The labourers are many in the world; the workers are less in number. But the third variety is very few indeed in the world at a given period of history, and they are called **"Men of achievement"**. Thus, men of labour, men of work and men of achievement – is the threefold classification of the Ṛṣis. Ask the man of achievement: "What is it that you want in the world? Why are you working? O Buddha, why did you work? O Christ, why did you work? O Mohammed, why did you move from place to place preaching, against many odds?" Surely, they were working in the world not for wages, nor for anything else; but they must necessarily work because they feel such an urge that they must work and they work for fulfilment.

Such people work in the world, not for profit, nor for success, but with a feeling of 'kṛtakṛtyatā' with a sense "I have done the right thing to be done", and irrespective of the age, irrespective of whether we are going to recognize them in their lifetime or not. They are the men of achievement. All that a man of achievement wants is that secret joy in himself, that sense of fulfilment "I did what best I could do in that matter". Whether others recognize it or not, they do not care at all and invariably generations crushed them down in all periods of history. Christ was destroyed. Almost all great men from the ancient times up to our own Mahatma Gandhi were mercilessly murdered. The world did crush them out but they died most happily because of the sense of overflowing joy that comes from the thought, "So long as I lived in the world I did the right thing, and got my generation to do the right thing. Whether others valued it or not, it is their destiny indeed, but I have done my job as best as I could." In that ecstatic joy they invariably die. All such people are indeed called **"Men of fulfilment"**.

The men of fulfilment, when they worked in the world outside, did not work for feathering their own home for a more comfortable life; nor did they work in the world outside for bringing a heaven upon earth, but they worked among men shoulder to shoulder. By practice and precept they tried to lead mankind to live the ideal life. More often than not such men were persecuted by either the state or the society, for they were too idealistic for their age. Against all such obstacles, the man of fulfilment lived on, inspiring other by his joyous ways of life and thus brought about a new movement of moral upheaval in the country. Thus the morality, the culture and the civilization of the society always rose up because of the work of this mighty man, in his short span of life. A Christ lived only 30 years in the world. A Vivekānandā lived only about 37 years in the world and Śaṅkara had a span of only 32 years. All of them gave a push and fillip to the ideal, a life that they themselves lived and experienced, not merely conceived and talked about.

Thus, all men of achievement are not mere labourers nor are they workers but, they are seekers of fulfilment. By living in the world, in the society, the idealistic life, in spite of the fact that the people around them were not living nor willing to live the life-ideal, they thrilled and inspired their generation, generating in them awe and a reverence for the perfect life. Such ideal men alone, have crowbarred the world to a higher level, to a greater consciousness of the moral principle.

Today we hear from most of the educated people and the great workers in the secretariat: "Swamiji, we cannot afford to be honest in the secretariat." "How sad, my boy!" Of course, I know the difficulty. It needs a hero to create beauty in the country or progress in the country. It is not with the coward. If you are not ready to make sacrifices, no country can come forward. You cannot expect a miracle to happen, a great angel to come down to the country and suddenly with a touch and magic power, make the entire country glow up.

It is by individual sacrifices alone, that this is possible. Everywhere in all fields; political, economic and cultural, progress has taken place in the world only because of such sacrifices. If you, a few people, after realizing the glow of life and 'Right way of living' and the 'Art of existence' were to enter into the secretariat and live an ideal moral standard of living, finding fulfilment in work itself, not caring for the petty earnings, I tell you that you will be inspiring the others there to know this new way of life. Until you are ready to make that sacrifice, the throttling, blood curdling, vicious circle of corruption that has come into our government cannot be removed. You cannot solve the problem by saying, "What can we do? The whole system is like that, Swamiji!" So long as you remain there saying that the system is like this, do you think that the poor labourer, the poor taxpayer in the village, is held responsible? Can he do anything to improve the organization? It rests upon our shoulders to improve our own houses. Your neighbour is not going to come to improve relations between you and your wife and children. Each one has to understand and live the right life in the home, and the home is beautified. Since we have taken upon ourselves this great mission in life and have entered the secretariat, it is necessary that each one must understand that in our little social status, little field, whether at home or in our society or in the institution where we are working, we must have at least the integrity in ourselves, so that we will be able to work in the world outside with a sense of achievement rather than for a mere flippant, passing honour of success, or for a little more money in our pocket.

Thus, there are three types of activities in the world coming from three types of people. The labourer is the first category. We call him a labourer who is working in the world just for wages. And what does he want the wages for? For fattening his own body, for giving comfort to his wife and children. Beyond that, even to help a neighbour is impossible for him. What he wants is, wages. Even if this idea comes to the greatest man in the country, he is only a labourer. Our respect for him immediately ceases. The nation no longer looks up to such a man. The nation no longer looks up to that group or company. No more can they lead because we understand the hollowness of their activity.

The second variety is those who struggle hard in the world outside because every one of them has great enthusiasm and great vision in life. They are ready to starve, and are ready to suffer. The spiritual missionaries, the great cultural thinkers, are all struggling on to bring the ideals they have got into the world.

The best among them are indeed, very very rare. They do not generally come in every generation. It is they who give a fillip to the general cultural beauty of society and they crowbar the entire generation, lift the entire society to a higher standard of life, a higher dignity of morality, a greater virtue of life. Such mighty men are called saints and Seers or Avatāra Puruṣas in our country, great prophets in foreign countries or incarnations of great virtues and values.

They are called so, not because they worked in the world, or because they had a great party, but because they lived the ideal life. Each one, inspired the others even after the body was annihilated. The fragrance of their thought, the might and glory of their ideals gather new momentum as the years roll by. The more the generations come after the date of their death, the more seems to be the compelling charm and the beauty in which they lived. Christ died two thousand years ago and yet you find that the farther you move away from the ideal that he lived for, and he met joyously his own death at the hands of that generation, his glory is becoming more and more compelling in the world. 2,500 years ago the Buddha died; the more we move away historically from him, the more detachedly we can experience what he did, and we appreciate the Prince of Compassion more and more.

No doubt, if there were newspaper men at the time of the Buddha, or Christ, both of them would have been given only a corner in the eighth page of the newspaper saying that the criminal Christ also has been murdered, or that the Buddha died as an unknown fellow during his retreat. "He was, once upon a time, the great prince Siddhārtha, but the fool left everything like a stupid person, went into retreat, begged in the streets of Sārnath where he lived until he died, and 1000 disciples of his are knocking about all over. He was only a manufacturer of beggars in the country." That would have been the report of our own local representative of the newspaper, if there were newspaper at that time. They never issued statements to the press or held conference of the press. They silently, quietly and secretly worked in their own villages, and in their own streets. Like Socrates, calling on the villagers around and singing about the new vision of thought, they lifted their generation to a higher level.

In our cities we see the sight of people going about the coffee-houses and having a jolly good time. Jolly good time cannot be had if jolly good money is not there and the jolly good money to all the millions of people can never be given by any government.

Everybody in the secretariat has told me "Swamiji, it is very difficult." "What is very difficult?" I asked, "To make both ends meet" is the reply. I said "Why? You have been getting a good salary now." "Swamiji, you do not know; nowadays, it is very difficult to make both ends meet." Now when I heard this from a clerk, I thought probably the fellow was poorly paid and, therefore, this answer, I went to the upper division clerk, and he too told me 'very difficult to make both ends meet'. So, I went to the superintendent, he also said "Swamiji, these days, you do not know, it is very difficult to make both ends meet." The deputy secretary, undersecretary, the secretary, the minister, the chief minister; go to any one, everyone says, "It is very difficult to make both ends meet."

Now, what is the matter? Why this is so? The more you get, the more difficulties arise to make both ends meet. It is all because our stomach has got a knack; it looks, of growing farther than our belt. Take any belt you purchase, by the time you come home from Chandni Chowk* and try it, the stomach is bigger, and the ends of the belt do not meet! We have to learn to keep our stomach in parity, so that the belt may be sufficient to cover it or else the whole life or the twenty-four hours in a day will not be sufficient to fatten the body or the stomach. So if your stomach grows bigger, then something must be done and today the modern man, whether he is a capitalist or an ordinary man, seems to think that the stomach has grown so big now that the entire head is inside it. The stomach has become so big that there is nothing beyond the stomach - the head also is a stomach, the heart also is a stomach! Nothing goes beyond the stomach, because the stomach has become so big that the appetite to live the sensuous life has become insatiable.

How will he be able to work? A man who is a great sprinter, one who is good at running and wants to become an Olympian, needs agility of body; he must keep his physical body in good shape. With a growing stomach he cannot be a sportsman in life. He cannot even move about properly.

---

* Name of a place in Delhi

We think that intellectually we have become so potbellied, and have got so much to satisfy that even the two hands, two legs and twentyfour hours around the clock seem to be not sufficient. There is, therefore, disgruntlement at all times and discontentment in the heart. A man who is riddled with discontentment cannot act beautifully in the world outside. He cannot have a greater vision in life, continuously working in the world outside.

When I was a student at Lucknow, I went once to meet Mr. Sapru. He was the greatest man at that time in the field of law. He asked me, "Young man, what do you want?" I said, "Sir, I am student of law in this university." 'Hm', he said, with a grandfather like dignity, "Acha (ok), sit down", I sat down. "What do you want?" he asked, as he was looking through his glasses (you know the frightening look of the aged people). I said, "All that I want from you Sir, is the secret of your success in your profession. I am going to enter your profession and I would like to know this." He looked at me rather piercingly and said, "Look, my son, I think you will never be a successful lawyer".

"This is very unfair, Sir, because I am just now coming to the second year, how dare you say that?"

"No, my boy, you cannot. Your clothes and your entire attitude, I think, are not good."

"I will try to change, but will you please tell me the secret?"

I said, "How did you come to the height, what is the secret of it?"

He told me, "The secret of becoming successful in the world, and if you want to take my place in the world, there is only one method; **"Live like a hermit, work like a bull, work like a horse"**. He corrected himself, because the bull is not swift. He continued, "For the last twenty-two years, would you believe it my dear boy, I have never seen a picture, not because I cannot afford it, but I have no time to see picture." Sir C.V.Raman also said that he had not seen a picture. Which is the club that Mr. Nehru is visiting nowadays? Where is time for these things for such men of success, men of action?

Take any man of success in any profession, he has no time to waste in the coffee-house, no time, even to go near the picture-houses. But most of the people, if they have a little time at their disposal, go round and round the Connaught Place,* polishing the verandahs. They have nothing to crave for, to demand, to work, to achieve for themselves. All that they want is to live at the flesh-level. Such men are to be counted with animals only, because the animal also lives always at the flesh level, either it eats, or licks, or mates.

---

* Name of a place in Delhi

If man also remains at that level only, he will live only an animal life, and in the animal kingdom, happiness and prosperity and peace can never be, because they are not the destiny of animals.

Prosperity, culture and progress are possible not merely because you are physically a human being, but only if you are human in your mind and intellect. If you do not attain this great human stature within your intellect, then national progress is impeded, the general progress of the country is impeded, and you and I shall weep on and on, quarrelling with everybody, with every government that might come in the country, and die away in sorrow and tears alone, never gaining that joy of having lived.

In order to live and to bring out the maximum happiness from ourselves, to work out the best for ourselves, everyone of us must have a goal in life, a mission, an inspiring ideal; looking up to that ideal and hitching our eyes to it, we must work on in the world outside. Thereby, the work becomes chastened; the work itself become its own reward for the individual and a great joy wells up in his mind, not in terms of what he gets on the first of the month, but what he gives to the society as best as he can, from the place where he is.

THE SECRET OF ACTION (Talk II)

Yesterday, we tried to find out the inevitability of action, how action cannot but be, because action in the world outside is the expression of the individual life. A dead carcass can afford to live without action. Any living organism, if it is to live, must necessarily act in the world outside. According to the type of action that we put forth, the great thinkers of the past divided activity into three types. They said that there are men of action who fall under the category of 'labourers' and the activity emerging out from such individuals is only for the purpose of wages, for the purpose of making themselves more comfortable. The very activity emerging out of them becomes, not labour, but work if only they have a greater vision of life and try to translate that vision into the world outside.

You and I are also working, the greatest scientists are also working, the great philosophers are working, a labourer on the roadside is also working. All of us are taking out so much of perspiration from the body; so much of effort is being put in, and yet the quality of work will depend upon the quality of intention as well as the quality of the mind and intellect behind.

If the individual who is putting forth effort is having a self-centred view,"I am working so that I may get wages or some profit or some little return with which I am going to benefit myself or benefit my wife and children"; the effort of such an individual is merely labour, mere sweat and toil. The very labour becomes more divinised, more glorious (the effort put forth remaining the same), if the mind has got a better vision of life, an inspiring goal. Then the effort becomes work.

Thirdly, the highest type of individuals, working in the world outside, are called men of achievement. They work not merely as labourers or workers, not for the sake of wages, nor for the sake of success; they have no intention of making life happier, or of bringing any goal into the world. They live and act seeking only a sense of fulfilment.

All of us have only twentyfour hours per day. Whether one is a mighty man who is making history in the world, or a man who is earning his livelihood, this is true. After twentyfour hours the next day comes; to a man of achievement, to a great scientists discovering, to a poet writing, to an immortal artist painting and to an ordinary labourer working. Three hundred and sixtyfive days make a year. Yet, you find that the men who make history within a short time of ten to twenty years, carry out such a wonderful achievement as to leave behind something remarkable for which the succeeding generations are grateful. Often, it is a wonder to many as to how one ordinary individual within a short time could do so much work. They contribute so much to the world while there are others with him, working much harder than him, but leaving nothing behind.

When we act, the glory of action is dependent upon, not the environment, not where you work and how you work, but it is the intention or motive behind the work that lends enchantment to the very work. The work is glorified, it gathers a new momentum, it is bristling with a new ardour, only because of the ardency or the faithful intentions of the heart behind the worker's hand. Take sculpture, after all there are so many sculptors, some of them working upon some Rajah, some on a political leader, some on fairies standing in the parks. Now, look at the beautiful sculptures in the temples or churches. The sculptor here not only did the form, but his heart had a great love and reverence to the theme that he was working on. Such sculptured pieces become immortal in the world. It is no more a stone, chiselled by iron bits. The pieces start talking. The individual seems to have poured his personality and beauty of heart into the pieces of stone. They are not mere silicon dioxide or mere rock pieces, but they seem to give the immortal message of the heart of the sculptor. It is the same in painting and writing.

THE SECRET OF ACTION (Talk II)

This is the burden of yesterday's talk, inevitability of work. Work cannot but be. The quality of work seems to be dependent upon not only the field where we are working, not only the way we are working, not only the theme on which we are working, but also on the ardour and sincerity, the intention, the great motive or ideal that has inspired our heart when we are at work. If this much has been understood, I may say, now something about the very mechanism of action.

How are we acting? What do we mean by action? Today we are all students of science, and so we are not ready to accept an idea for granted, however noble it might be, unless we know the intricate mechanism in it. If you purchase a radio set and keep it at home, and if you have a 14 year old son, by evening you may rest assured that the set will have to go back to the mechanic. Why? Because, he wants not merely to hear music, but to know how it works. Therefore, he tries to dismantle it with his penknife, and then he finds he cannot assemble it back. Now you cannot blame that boy, even though momentarily you feel disappointed and you may blame him. But you are satisfied that the boy is mechanically minded. The boy wants to know what it is all about. This is the very spirit of the modern age. Therefore, when the teachers or the scriptures try to explain that there is work, and that its quality will depend upon the beauty of emotion behind it, we are not ready to accept it. We want to know how these are connected together. Therefore, a little knowledge of the instruments of action, and how they act on in the world outside is unavoidable and must necessarily follow. If one such mechanism of man as a dynamic creature working in the world outside is understood, the rest will automatically follow. How the greater ideal will inspire the man to work better will be clear.

When a living creature is living in a field, you all know that the external stimuli are reaching it. They are called the form, the colour, the smell, the taste and the sound. These five different types of stimuli known as indriya-viśayas reach us. Just now, you are hearing me; but not merely hearing. Everybody if lifting his head, because he wants to see me also. Thus, you are not only hearing but also seeing. Thus through your ears and eyes I am entering into your bosom. Not a single second can you remain in the world without receiving some stimuli. Whether you like it or not, the stimuli reach your bosom through five different avenues or inlets known as the senses. Through the eyes only the form enters; through the ears only the sound enters; through the nose only the smell enters; through the tongue only the taste and through the skin only touch enters. These are called the sense organs. Thus, through the sense organs the various objects of the world enter into me, inviting me to reach to them.

THE SECRET OF ACTION (Talk II)

As all of these reach the man, the instrument or mechanism within man that receives them from the various windows of reception and makes them into a file; that receiving clerk is called the mind. If your mind wanders to some other idea, you cannot hear at all. A bosom friend of mine may come in front of me and say 'Hello', I may not 'Hello' him back at all. My physical body is here and the friend is standing in front. My eyes are wide open, and yet I may not see him. You tell your friend that you are worried, and therefore, you did not see him. If you are worried, you do not see, because your mind is engaged with the worry, and, therefore, you are not there to receive the stimuli. It invariably happens. If the sense organs are receiving the stimuli, the instrument that is receiving the stimuli is called the mind. It is the reception clerk in the inner secretariat.

When the mind thus receives the stimuli, it cannot dispatch the file immediately. It has to be put up to higher authorities for final decision. The mind cannot come to a decision, it can only receive the stimuli. The higher authority is called the intellect, the judging faculty. The intellect will judge how I am to react to this situation and what I am to do. The orders or the final decisions come from the intellect.

The intellect also cannot judge it haphazardly as it wills. It is not a tyrannical rule, it is the rule of law that obtains in the secretariat. The intellect can judge one way or the other, but the intellectual judgment of a particular case will depend upon the standing rules and precedents of the department. These existing rules and precedents of the department, already in the intellect, colour our judgment and are called the vāsanās, or impressions of the past experiences.

The past experiences would control, direct, regulate and discipline my present reaction to the world outside, because my intellectual judgment will be coloured by its own immediate past experiences. Thus, if a bottle of whiskey is seen by a devout Brahmin and a drunkard, the latter runs towards the bottle while the former runs away from it. The bottle itself did not attract or repel them. It is the type of intellect of the man that determines the attraction towards it or repulsion from it.

Thus, the ideas and ideals that we are already having in our intellect condition the intellect in judging how it should tackle the stimuli that have been received by the mind and put to the intellect to judge. The outer world enters through the sense organs into the mind, the mind puts up the received stimuli to the intellect, the intellect judges them according to the existing vāsanās that control the intellect, and when the judgment is passed, the order or the file is sent back again to the mind. The mind is not only a receiving clerk but also a dispatch clerk. It creates economy in the inner secretariat, so that the receiving clerk and the dispatch-clerk are one and the same person. According to the orders passed by the intellect, the mind regulates the proper muscles to act in the world outside. All of this happens instantaneously.

It is up to the intellect to come to a judgment. But, how I will judge the situation is different from how you will judge the situation. Our judgments will be different, because the ideas and ideals that I am inspired by and those under which you are working, and the various vāsanās under which he is working. All of these are different from individual to individual. Therefore, the reactions of individuals are different from moment to moment. Every individual acts differently under same circumstances. It is only because of the type of ideals with which we are working in the world outside. I repeat. The external world in the form of stimuli enters into me. I cannot enter your bosom because there is no accommodation. You all cannot enter into me as such because there is no accommodation; but you enter me only in the form of stimuli. When the stimulus comes into me, it is received by my mind. The mind immediately sends it to the intellect. The intellect with its past experiences understands and shows how I must respond to the stimulus. One responds to the situation or to the world nobly, another ignobly. It is not because of the world, not because of the environment, not because of the body or mind, but because of the type of ideals in both of them.

Supposing now in the Connaught Place you saw a man walking in front of you. He had worn the latest type of American pants, which had a hip pocket. In the hip pocket, the fool had put his purse and the purse fell down. You saw this. The fellow had his thoughts elsewhere and was not aware of the falling of the purse. Now, all that has happened is this. A purse of a gentleman has fallen in front of you. You take the purse in hand and realize that it is heavy and it is the first of the month. The chance is yours. You think: "Shall I put it in my pocket? There is nobody to see me. Shall I do so, or shall I call the fellow: Buddhoo,* come here, there you are, your purse. In what way should I respond?" You have complete freedom, either to arrogate it to yourself or call the man and give it to him. Now what decides your reaction? Your own intentions, your ideals and education, which you have already in you. If, at that time your negative tendencies are forcing you more and more, the purse goes quietly into your pocket and you try to justify saying: "Dekho,** for the last one month I have been crying to Bhagvān to help me somehow or other, honest men are always protected by Bhagvān . When he wants to give, he gives it on the footpath of Connaught Place!

---

* Stupid
** See

Thus, you justify yourself. If you are a cultured man of real education and real understanding of life, you immediately see the tragic picture of this man returning home to his young wife and children, having lost his purse. It is a painful scene indeed. You get the idea "Let me help him. Ordinarily, I cannot afford to give in charity so much money but here is his own money, which is certainly a charity if I now give it back. Hey Nārāyaṇa,, you have given me a chance of helping him, and therefore, I will call the loser and give the purse to him" Before he could say, 'thank you', you disappear, and with a growing sense of having done something wonderful, you go out into the wide world.

Everything depends upon the type of ideas in our mind. The way in which we behave in the world is altered, controlled, regulated, and commanded, by the type of ideals that inspire us in our actions in the world. So the question is, "How I may act in the world, how I can improve my actions and gain a greater achievement in life." This cannot be done by working double shift. That is the idea of the modern, material, commercial world, that if I work double, I can do double the quantity. When a machine can work six hours, it can produce a certain quantity. If it can work twelve hours, it can produce double the quantity, it is admitted. But a man's work in society is not measured by the hours that he is working. It is not the quantity of action that matters but the quality. The quality of action is improved by the ideals, which illumine and inspire the individual worker in the world outside. Thus, the nobler the ideal the greater the shine and beauty of action, and such ideals that inspire me at all times to bring out of myself a better efficiency, and beauty of action are called noble ideals or moral ideals. Ideals that bring me to a dispirited and dejected attitude to such an extent that my actions, however efficient they are, ultimately tumble down to doom and sorrow and failure at all times, such ideals are false or immoral ideals.

So the ideals that inspire me positively and chasten the labour are called noble ideals. The spirit of freedom, the spirit of reverence to your country, the spirit of sacrifice for the sake of society, are all inspiring ideals. Under such ideals, mighty men have done great, ennobling activity in the world and fruits of their actions are enjoyed by the future generations for many years. So the higher the ideal that inspires an individual, the nobler is the action that he does in the world outside.

After all, to enter with a concealed dagger in your coat, to jump over the walls of a private house to cut off the bars of a window, to move stealthily forward into the house, to see whether anybody is awake by watching the rhythm of the sleeping persons, then to go to your victim, to plunge the dagger into that man, murder him and quietly, stealthily and successfully to retire from the scene into the road, all this is no joke. It is a huge task indeed. It calls for many vital qualities of the individual personality to do it efficiently. But what is the product of all this intelligence, smartness, courage and heroism? One member of the society is dead, and I, the murderer, thought, "That rascal is out of the world and I shall be happy." But from that day onwards I start finding that I am not at all happy. On the other hand, my peace and tranquillity are broken, because of the reactions that come into my mind. My best qualities are put forth in a piece of work inspired by negative thought. The goal in my mind is false, and even though the work is successfully accomplished, it is only a sad act of callous murder.

You are all working in various departments. You enter the secretariat, which is the centre of the whole administration of a progressive country. However, when each individual is bending over his work on that little table, if the deal is not good, the work will not ultimately succeed. That is exactly what is happening with our plans. Our first, second and third five-year plans are wonderful. The best engineers, greatest thinkers and workers are working on projects. Ultimately, when the minister comes to open the dam, it is found that water cannot flow through the canals, because the canals are a few feet above the water level. The work is no doubt accomplished, but something in the quality of work is lacking.

Our Śāstras say, that work can bring forth real enduring result, not merely because of the quantity of work put forth, but by the quality of inspiration under which man has undertaken the work. The greater the ideal, the brighter is the action and the product.

The beauty of the action we are doing, increases when the ideal on which we are working is noble and great. A Mahatma Gandhi was only a Barrister-at-Law, a Gujarati Barrister. He probably would have been a 'successful one' if he had only looked after his wife and children. But, what would have been the total turnover of his work? On the other hand, the same individual, the same physical entity, when he was inspired by the ideal of his country's freedom, was a different person, a Mahatma. Even if he had failed to bring about our present day freedom, the historians cannot avoid mentioning him as a great soul. It is because of the change in the moral vision of the country and of all the thinkers of the world that he brought about, and the quality of work that he turned out. The quality of it has been higher and nobler because of the high ideals that inspired him.

The Buddha, the Prince of Compassion, could work so beautifully and his work is not forgotten by anyone. There are very many pundits* in Benares and Sāranath, and very many Bhikṣus** functioning in the

---

* Educated men
** Beggars

world, but their names are not coming out. We are not feeling indebted to them much, because the inspiration and ideals with which they are working are not so noble and serene. The nobler the ideal, the greater you and I shall discover the efficiency coming out of ourselves.

Now think, suddenly you hear that your house is on fire. You rush therein, and find that the entire house is in flames, and the fire brigade is standing helpless. At that time you find your wife walking out of the fire with a child in hand. When you make enquiries, you hear, spellbound, the thrilling news that the child was sleeping upstairs in a room. In the panic everybody ran, helter-skelter, and then the mother remembered the child. They asked the fire brigade man to save the child. That man in spite of his forty years experience said "Mā, no human being can go inside. The whole thing is ablaze." The mother immediately forgets everything, and in a hysterical ecstasy she runs into the fire. Everybody is expecting that she would come out like a pakora***. On the other hand you find that not even her sari was burnt. She rushes to the room, takes the child and comes out. After this incident, tell her to go near the fire, and she is afraid. Her efficiency has gone, but under the inspiration of that great love for her child, she could do miracles. If that is the potentiality of the human mind, can't she live twenty-four hours of the day as a heroine? She

*** A popular fried eatable.

cannot, because she has not got that inspiring goal. So an ordinary man may be a coward, but when he is inspired by a great ideal, you find, that out of himself, he pulls out miraculously a new stream of energy and vitality.

Supposing now, God forbid, your wife is seriously ill. You have no more leave available. She is ill at home and you are working in the office. Your sister is called to look after your wife during the day. You take your turn in the evening and night. You serve your wife all the night. For months together you do not have a chance of going to sleep. Out of sheer love for your wife, you do not feel tired. From her sick bed she says "Darling, you go to bed, please sleep; you have to work in the daytime, it is my prārabdha,* I will suffer; you may sleep, please." The man replies that he is not feeling sleepy at all. After one month of twentyfour hours everyday, the man says he is not feeling tired.

How is it that this much of energy came out of him? Ordinarily it is admitted that by 5 o'clock we are tired, not because we did anything, but because we are tired. Now on the other hand, when my wife or child is ill, out of my love for them I discover in myself new energy, which no medical man or health minister can explain. We discover it in ourselves. If that much

---

* Luck

of energy and efficiency are there concealed in ourselves, what is the secret mechanism by which we can take them out?

Discovering a goal or vision in life, a great ideal to inspire, surrounding oneself to that ideal, and working in the world outside seems to be the secret of discovering new dynamism in our activities. We thereby raise the very standard of activity in us and thus bring about a greater happiness in the world outside. That goal each one will have to discover. There was a time when the goal was dharma or religion. Today it is not. I do not think that merely an ideal of God or the ideal of 'Virāta Nārāyaṇa' is sufficient to inspire. Therefore, we like to take up an active and creative thought for the country and society. This seems to be actively occupying our mind. So to serve the country and to serve a huge nation like ours, which is as backward as it is now, each one will point alone. Each one will have to shoulder at his own place. The typist is a typist, the clerk is a clerk, the superintendent, the politician, everyone will work on. Thus you will convert your own little table or corner of activity as a Vṛndāvan where you are playing with that mighty Lord who is the destiny of the country and who guides it all times, each one going about his work with as much serious nerve and ability as possible with a vision of a noble country and progressive nation in himself. You alone can discover a new spurt of energy and enthusiasm in yourself.

I am not suggesting this only to the secretariat workers. This is true for the factory man, the industrialist also. If the selfish industrialist thinks that he will make all the money and leave it to his wife and children, he is thoroughly mistaken. In that spirit no country can grow independent. He should think that he is to produce more for the benefit of society. With that ideal, when he is working, the political or economic salvation of the country is possible. Think, your own ideals of work become chastened. The individual thereby gains an immense amount of reward, not in terms of cash, not in terms of money returned by the society, but in the spirit of a joy that arises out of a bosom which has done the action rightly at the right time.

I will talk about this joy of action, joy of achievement in the next lecture.

JOY – THE REWARD OF ACHIEVEMENT (Talk III)

On the opening day we tried to find out the inevitability of action. Action itself, is an expression of life and therefore all of us, so long as we live, cannot avoid action. And yet, while acting according to the intention and purpose, with which individuals act in the world, acts of man can fall under three categories, **sheer labour, inspiring work, achievements.** In all these three types of work, whether it is low or high, the work as such is one and the same, but the enduring results will come only when we are acting with the attitude of a man of achievement.

Yesterday, we tried to find out, in case there is the inevitability of action, how best am I to act on? How do we act? What makes me act, what are the personality layers that come to express themselves in action? If once I know this mechanism of action, then I probably will understand the technique and the art of adjusting my personality in such a way as the action of mine may fall under these highest types of activities, activities that bring about achievement for me as well as for the society. When, I then analyse and try to understand the mechanism of action, I find that the external world of stimuli through the sense organs are received by the mind, and the mind puts up these stimuli for the intellect to judge. The intellect judges it, according to the vāsanās that it has got (the ideas that the intellect has already gathered in it) and thus the intellect orders the type of responses with which I must meet the challenges of the world.

The responses that come out of me are called actions. In order that the action may manifest through me while I am living, it is necessary that the world of stimuli must reach my personality through my sense organs and when they come out of my personality, there is action from me.

So, every action of an individual is his response to the external challenge. A dead man is no more acting because the dead body is no more receiving any challenge from the outer world. No stimuli can reach him. So long as we are alive, the challenge must necessarily reach us. Wherever there is a challenge that is received by us, our intellect must, rightly or wrongly, respond to the world outside. The responses are not in our control at this moment, because they are according to the type of education or the type of vāsanās that I have already gathered.

As I told you yesterday that in case I see that purse on the footpath, the question is whether I am to return it to him or put in my own pocket. At that moment a man who is putting it his pocket cannot be blamed.

We cannot ask, i.e. "Why have you done it?" It is clear that he got only one instruction for himself: "Pocket it, why do you worry about it? That is a fool who has lost it. You are intelligent because you got it, it is yours." A hundred arguments like this are given by the intellect and if you are morally a good man, immediately the very same intellect would argue a thousand other arguments for the same instance and you will say, "That man's worry will be terrible, when he goes home, he will be in despair. So let me call him and give it to him. Even though it is his own purse, when I give it to him, he gains a joy as if I have given him a charity of that much of amount, let me enjoy it and let me enjoy the joy of his smile." Now, both of these are reactions to one and the same challenge, but in one intellect there is only one way of reacting to it **"let me put it in my pocket". Another reaction is, "let me give it back to him".**

With external challenges remaining the same, different individuals seem to reach to them differently and their reactions are their actions, as we call them. One individual acting in the world outside bumps into achievement and success, while another individual in the same field of world is reacting to it so unintelligently that he is bumping downwards to disastrous sorrows. No doubt you and I immediately and blandly say, "The world is a bad place". You would like to curse somebody for your failure, just as a bad worker will always say, "My instrument was not good". (In fact his work was bad and he wanted to justify himself by saying that the instrument was bad). Similarly, the majority of us are escapists from life and when we are meeting with failure we want to attribute our failure to a cause somewhere outside, "It is so because nobody was helping me, it is because the world has not given me a good chance in life, it is because of the environment, etc." But essentially, when we analyse a human personality, we shall find that if I am failing, if my actions are bringing about more unhappiness to myself and the world, it is not because of the world but because of my own false and wrong responses to the challenges from the world.

In the Mahābhārata war, we find that Kṛṣṇa was also facing Duryodhana, Arjuna was also facing Duryodhana. Both of them were facing the same challenge. Both were facing the war and yet we find Kṛṣṇa smiling with the joy of confidence, while Arjuna becoming hysterical, falling down from the chariot to say: "I cannot fight, I do not know what I am to do; which is right and which is wrong. Am I to fight or am I not to fight?" Here is the same challenge of war, but one faces it joyously, while another gets hysterical about it. In these cases we find that it is not the challenge that is bad. It is the man who has the capacity that acts properly. He who gives himself over to some negative tendencies like fear acts wrongly.

Successes and failures are our own successes and failures, not of the world outside. The same situation, the same sun, moon and the stars, the same climatic conditions, the same flora and fauna, the same town is available for all of us. But I fail in the town and become a tragic man of the village, while you become a successful man in the same village. How is it possible? It is only because I know not how to meet my challenges and to react properly, while you know how to react to them and therefore are able to make the environment conducive to your own development and growth.

We find that the responses of an individual will depend upon the type of ideas and ideals he has; the higher the ideals, the greater the inspiration to act on, in the world. This ideal, every individual discovers for himself. Nobody can give it. A great painter, an artist, or a scientist, a freedom fighter, a political leader – all of them have their ideals. To the extent we can faithfully live up to the great ideals, dedicate ourselves to the ideals more and more, a good column of energy seems to spring forth from our hearts and we are able to apply that energy into activity, pursuing our ideas.

Thus, everyone must necessarily have an ideal. If that vision of your goal of life is nothing more than, "I must have a comfortable life; my body must be fattened; I must have good food, clothing and shelter;

my wife and children must be happy," then that goal is so low that there is no inspiration at all.

If you ask a hundred young men who are working here, why have you joined the secretariat, etc., every one of them, without an exception, will say "It is all 'Pet ke vaste', for belly's sake." Beyond that there is no goal in life; to fill the stomach or to look after my wife and children is the maximum goal that we have got this moment and when you aim at this goal, you are exhausted, tired and weary.

Friends, I meet often very many secretariat people. Their general complaint is "Swamiji, there is no time to study, there is no enthusiasm to study anything, no enthusiasm to live a higher life." Why? "Because, we are exhausted by the time we come back from the secretariat. Pitiable is the condition of the secretariat clerk. We are living far away. Early in the morning we cycle up the distance, or we go by a bus, and we have to stand in a queue, and by the time we reach the secretariat and come back late in the evening, Swamiji, there is no energy at all in us because of the exertion of work."

Go to a village, observe the farmer working from the morning onwards till late in the evening. He comes home, takes a bath, has his dinner, and thereafter he takes his drum and the singing and dancing of the village folks goes on until midnight. Smiling and laughing, he is hale and hearty, he is not at all tired. Being scientifically minded, let us analyse how much energy that you and I in the secretariat spend as against the farmer in his field. When analysed, we meet with an amazing contradiction!

Take an individual who is working in the secretariat. Early in the morning he gets up at six o'clock, and then what happens? He says "as soon as I get up, I am worried because my tea was not given in time. After the tea, Swamiji, I went and took my bath and washed myself, then I had to go to the bazaar and get the vegetables and come back." Very good, how far was the vegetable market? "One and half furlongs away." Very good, you brought the vegetables. "Then they cooked the food. I ate the food, and then I had to dress myself and go to the bus stand." "How far away is the bus stand?" "One furlong." All right, one furlong you walked and stood there in the line. When the bus came, you stood inside the bus. The bus took you to the secretariat. You got down and went upstairs to your room and there the secretariat clerk says, "I am tired already". In an air-cooled room, or a room, which is water-cooled properly, and a ceiling-fan going on terribly, there you say, "I am tired". Then, he goes to the canteen for refreshment with a hot cup of coffee. Revived, you come back to your seat. Then, "let me have a cigarette". So back you go to the verandah of the canteen, have a cigarette, and then come back to your room. But by the time you go there and take out the file, it is already lunchtime, not yet exactly, but coming closely. Then you go for another two cups of coffee and tiffin. Finished, evening has come. What is the work done? Four letters, got typed or typed yourself. There you are, four little pieces have been sent out of which you definitely know that there are unnecessary queries! This is the work turned out, honestly speaking, and you come, again of course, standing in the queue and getting into the bus and then you say, you are tired, fatigued!

On the other hand, take the farmer. Early in the morning with a plough on his shoulder and two bulls standing in front of him, he goes to his plot of land – where is it? "Not one furlong away, but two and a half miles away". There he goes on ploughing from morning till noon, then he eats what he has brought with him in the morning, or what his son or daughter brought for him. He has been standing in the hottest sun. Ploughing is very strenuous indeed, and he gets exhausted. Up to three o'clock he takes rest, and again from three he ploughs and at 5.30 with the bulls and the plough he comes back, walking two and a half miles. The amount of perspiration that he has brought out himself, the calories of physical energy that he has spent in the field, are incomparably larger then that of a clerk or an assistant in the secretariat! When he reaches home, the farmer takes a bath, takes his dinner, and goes to the Chabuthar,* sits on a charpoy,** and thereafter starts his song, in full-throated glee. He goes on and on with a joy of ecstasy and there he has a revelrous time the whole night! Where did he get that much of energy?

If human beings have got that much energy, where is that energy going from us?

When you are saying that you are tired, my friends, I am not trying to prove that you are not tired. You are really tired. That farmer is not tired, because tiredness of life comes not because of physical exertion. Physical exertion cannot give you fatigue, and if at all there is fatigue, you rest half an hour, and the physical body will revive itself But the real fatigue that you and I, in the towns, feel is only the exhaustion of the mind. The moment the clerk got up in the morning, he was worried; worried of his tea, of his little room tenement, of his position, of his not getting more pay. Even in the bazaar he is worried because the vegetable merchant has got more money than he has. Whatever you see makes you worried. Somebody has got a cycle, you are worried that you have not one. Somebody has a Lambretta,*** you are worried. "Why should that rascal have the Lambretta?" Whenever

---

* Open place outside house.
** Wooden coir cot
*** Lambretta is a popular scooter.

anybody is going in a car, you are worried. Why? Because, he is going in a car. Therefore, you cross the road and make the car stop and wait until you cross the road. So much is your mental tension.

"I am worried, in a million ways, and by the time I go to the secretariat my energy has already ebbed out. When I see the superintendent, I am worried about him. I am worried about everybody including the peon in the secretariat who seems to be smiling more and more while I weep more and more in my mind." Thus, you get mentally exhausted, even though physically you have not done a lot of work. While in the case of the farmer, he thinks of his land and feels happy. When he ploughs with his bull, he feels happy because it is his bull. He walks two and half miles all the time dreaming. His legs are not touching the ground, for he is thinking of his smiling land. He ploughs on and on and each time he is ploughing physically he does get exhausted, but mentally he is in an ecstatic musical form. In the music of life itself, music of action. He is very happy in this thinking and therefore he is not at all exhausted. By the time he comes back and takes a bath in the evening he has revived himself and there is still a lot of energy in him.

This fatigue that we are feeling in the modern days is not the fatigue of the physical exertion, for the modern conveniences are such, as we need not spend our energy. To go upstairs, we need not spend energy because lifts are there. All over, we have comforts to economize our precious energy and yet we complain that we have no energy at all. It is all because of mental upset, which is the outcome of having no goal to aspire for or to keep in front of us. Our goal is "somehow or other go away from office, doing the least work and getting the maximum, and thinking how we can start the next strike so that we may get a little more for a little less work". This is all our thinking. When this negative thought comes, however much you are well looked after by the government, by your wife or father-in-law, still you will be the most unhappy man in the world!

A man's happiness depends not only upon the work in the field in which he is working, but also on his mental climatic conditions or his mental health. This mental health can be maintained, only when there is a greater goal in front of us to inspire us, and higher the goal the greater is the enthusiasm that inspires us. We discover new resources of energy welling up in ourselves, for our pouring out tirelessly into activity in the world. It is unavoidable that we must have a clearer and more creative goal in our life, so that we may look up to that goal and draw inspiration from it for our actions. When we have a goal in life such as the nation's prosperity, the country's progress, the goal itself inspires us, and the more it inspires us, the more we find the required energy for tireless activity.

KINDLE LIFE

As we even discover a goal and surrender ourselves to that goal in life, we hit upon a new column, an unknown column of energy within ourselves.

When I am talking to you, perhaps you have some intellectual perception of the ideal life and therefore you may surely feel inspired. But once the Swami is gone, the source of that inspiration is gone, you are back again in the good old way. Where was that energy gone? The energy was with us but it is dissipated into various channels and that water of energy is not available for the irrigation of activity.

We may build a dam and thereby discover a new column of water but, if this new column of water is not made use of and is not taken by the canals on both sides of the land, then the land cannot be cultivated properly. In order to make the land more arable we want water and for that purpose we have made the dam. By damming the river we have found a new column of water but this new column of water in the dam cannot create food, cannot create crops in the field, unless the canal system brings the water into the various fields and waters them properly. Similarly, by surrendering ourselves to a great goal, we find new enthusiasm and energy, but that enthusiasm or energy, if not properly channelised, either stagnates or dissipates into unnecessary channels and thus becomes unproductive.

This leakage of energy takes place, according to the great Ācāryas of the past, through three dissipating channels. The new energy, discovered by surrendering ourselves to a greater purpose in life, must be carefully preserved without dissipation. But in our present mental condition, no sooner do we find the energy than it dissipates through three leakages, very serious leakages indeed, so serious that whatever the quata of energy we have, it gets exhausted in no time. These leakages are to be blocked and the energy preserved. And if that is done, our activity or achievement or success is implicit and immediate. Now what are these leakages?

One of the main leakages is the 'Memories of the past'.

A very good student decided that he must get a first class and he went on studying for it but as the examination approached, he said, "I will be satisfied with a pass, I don't want this class", When asked "What happened?" He said "Never did I get a first class in the past; how can such a man as myself ever get a first class?" Thus the memories of the past means, "In the past I have always been an inefficient man; how can I be an efficient officer now?" Thus, the memories of the past come to disturb me and my new enthusiasm to live a nice life hereafter at least always oozes away, and I have no energy for any activity.

Another source of dissipation is 'Anxieties for the future'.

A boy who has always been a first class student wants to get in his M.A. examination, a rank in the university and the professors in his college are hopeful about him. The boy enters the examination hall rather pale-faced, and the professors think that it is because of over-study. When the question paper comes to him, he looks at it and swoons. The professor rushes to him, the boy says, "Give me some water". He is given water, he feels chakkar (reeling) and he wants to lie down. The professor is asking, "What is the matter?" The boy says, "Everything is lost". "What has happened?" asks the professor. The reply is: "How can I answer fourteen questions, even though I know their answers, when there is no time? My first class, rank, everything is gone!" The professor says "Fool, read again the question paper". The fellow reads the question paper once and again says, "Fourteen questions cannot be answered. Where is the time to answer all of them?" At last the professor must come and suggest a way out. (Nowadays the professor whispers into the ears of the students. In the good old days it was not allowed. Nowadays, you know, in Independent India everybody must help the other man). So the professor tells the boy to read the line in the question paper, which is printed in italics "Answer any three questions".

Because of his 'over anxiety' to work and get a first class, the boy's efficiency is lost and he wants only to run away from the examination hall. Many a student generally fails in the examination not because he has not studied but because of some such leakage of his dynamism, and his energy is dissipated and he becomes an empty man. Some of the students fail, although the entire university expected them to get a first class, while some of us pass, although nobody thought that we shall ever pass. We entered the examination with one certainty, that there is no chance of passing and so we quietly wrote on and thus there is some efficiency. The examiner thought, "Although the boy is rather backward, he is not too bad" and therefore he awards 35% of marks for us to pass through. Even such a person gets a third class while so and so fails. People say that one is a lucky man, and the other one is unlucky and so on. Actually there is no luck or ill luck. It all depends upon the mental equanimity with which you act in the world.

Thus the dissipation of our energies may take place either due to 'lingering memories of the past' or due to 'anxieties for the future'. When these two are renounced, the teachers say that there is a third way of dissipating leakage, which generally afflicts our administrators. That is the 'Excitement in the present'. In the secretariat you must be noticing that some officers are sitting from 8.00 a.m. to 8.00 p.m. and the peon comes and reminds them: "Sir, Bal bacche ghar me hain;* you may not go but I have to go home." The poor officer is sincerely doing work from morning till night. Yet the general impression about this administrator is that he is the most inefficient in his department. Everybody wants to avoid him. Now if you watch him working, it is a very interesting thing. He is honestly working no doubt, but he cannot come to any judgment. He looks right and left. Already on the table the files have piled up on both sides, he is worried about the heap of work. At that time the peon comes with another bundle of files and asks where it should be kept. By the time the officer takes up that file and tries to work he sees a red label coming out from a file, marked 'Immediate'. He is worried about it. So he closes down the file which he has half read. He pulls out the 'Immediate' file and starts reading it. By the time he finishes reading it, his mind harks back to the old file, while the peon has brought another bundle. He is worried, he is dejected. He knows not where to begin!

On the other hand, if he has got the idea that it is not one man's show, it is the whole country's administration, and that whatever file he takes up, it is better to close up all other ideas and concentrate upon the file, come to a decision and then keep that file away, then at least one is disposed off. If there are

---

* Children are at home (waiting for me).

one hundred files, only 99 are remaining. One by one if you are taking them without getting excited, then there will be efficiency in the activity itself. '**Excitement of the present**', brings our efficiency to zero and the man's energies are dissipated.

There are thus three outlets through which the energies go out; the regrets of the past, the unintelligent anxieties of the future, and the feverish excitement in the present.

The great Ācāryas have said that having discovered a great goal, surrender yourself to that goal and act towards it, drawing your inspiration from that goal, and thereby discover a new column of energy. Do not allow this energy to be dissipated in the futile memories of the past, regrets or failures, or in the imagined sorrows of the future, or in the excitement of the present. Thus, bring that entire energy focused into activity. That is the highest creative action in the world outside. Thereby the individual who is till now considered most inefficient finds his way to the highest achievement and success.

This is said very easily in a second. But in order to train our mind to this attitude, it needs consistent training because we have already trained the mind wrongly to such an extent that we have become perfect in imperfections! We have become masters in stupidity! Not knowing the art of action, we have been master artists in doing wrong things in life. When each individual is doing the wrong thing, the totality of activity will bring the country to a wrong end indeed.

If each one is given a car in the socialistic pattern, and nobody knows driving but everybody starts driving, what would be the condition on the road? Everybody has equal right on the public road. Then each car must necessarily dash against the other, and there is bound to be a jumble. This seems to be the very pattern of life that we are heading for. Every one of us is a vehicle. We know how to go forward. The point of intellect is very powerful and everyone is driving but nobody seems to know how to control the mental energy and direct it properly or guide it to the right destination.

Thus, there is too much of chaos in life; each one contradicts or drives against the other. All of them are intent on reaching a particular goal, but they reach nowhere and only end in disaster en route, because they know not how to control their minds, how to regulate their energies and pour them into activity.

When an individual has discovered new energy within himself, has learnt the art of stopping the dissipation, has learnt the art of fixing the entire energy to the piece of work in hand, a great joy called the 'Joy of the artisan' starts welling up .in his mind. The joy of the artisan or the artist is the joy that you can understand only when you experience it. An artisan or worker, working in the world outside and creating out of his work something new - may be a toy, may be a great instrument of precision, it does not matter what he is producing – his is the joy – the joy of having created something in the world.

No doubt to a large extent the mechanization of life in this machine age has robbed us of that joy that the artisan of the past had. In those days when they made an article of furniture or a piece of sculpture or painted a scene, they had a great joy that they did something creative. But nowadays the work is so much divided because of the mechanical intervention that man has been looted of his joy of creativity. It is because a blind, dead iron monster called the engine is producing everything. Furniture is produced by machinery; painting is replaced by photography, wherein the photographer has no joy of having produced it. All his joy is that he has adjusted his camera properly. Even when I find a good photo, I am not congratulating the photographer. I ask him what kind of camera he has used. The photographer comes and says that he has got a prize in the exhibition. We do not ask him what his techniques are. We only ask him what camera he is using and what kind of filters, etc. The glory of the prize is for the camera, but you being more intelligent than the camera, put the hand forward and got the prize; but in fact the camera should have got the prize because you have done nothing!

260

Thus everywhere, in anything that we produce we have no self-congratulation at this moment, because we produce nothing; the machine produces and we only attend to the machine that produces. To that extent no doubt the life and the joy of creation has gone away from our life.

But if we turn our attitude to a different angle, certainly even today that joy of having done the right thing in the right way can be had, if only we know how to turn your vision in right direction. For example, I am given a piece of work, say, typing, which is considered to be the most dreary work. If the typist executes his work neatly, without overtyping or mistake, he has his dividend of joy of having done something good.

We can discover our joy in the precision and perfection of the work that we turn out; whether others recognise it or not, we have got a satisfaction that we did our work as best as we could and there is silent stream of joy that sings a secret song at all times in our hearts. As a contrast to a clerk disappointed, and disgusted in the town, the great farmer working in the field is happy only because of the silent song of congratulation in his own mind.

Today in the modern world, whether it is in India or in the USA, the mental distraction and dissipation is so much that even though physically we may say they are well provided and happy, there is no happiness known to them. If you want to seek happiness through action, you must be able to discover this secret core of activity, this core of source of joy within ourselves, and if we can play upon these chords of musical beauty, then we can have the song of joy within ourselves, the joy that is in all achievements.

Thus, to sum up, according to the great Ācāryas, action can be good only when the actor, the individual, has got a great purpose or goal. Having gained that goal or ideal, for which we have concentrated all our education, whether it is a political or economic ideal, an ideal that you have chosen according to your own heart; it is not an ideal that somebody has given you, but that which is appealing to you most, then a new enthusiasm comes to you, and when there is enthusiasm, then sincerity, ardour and consistency of purpose automatically follow. Where there is no enthusiasm or inspiration, consistency of purpose can never be. Thus, once you have got a goal, something higher than yourself, your wife and children, your worldly comfort, etc., if there is a social vision, or a national vision that moves us forward, we discover within ourselves a new source of energy, and if this energy is not dissipated with the past memories, future anxieties or present excitement, i.e. if these three holes through which all the mental energy is leaking are blocked properly, the entire energy that we discovered within ourselves is available for focusing into the various activities that we are doing in the world. Activity is not performed merely by the hand. Where we are working with the hand, our heart and head also must be used. Thus, when the hand is working if the head and heart are present, there comes the artistic perfection.

All such artists, who have been able to work putting their head and heart where the hands are working, have discovered the joy of a samādhi, a joy of religious ecstasy, because where the physical, mental and intellectual personalities become integrated, the individual is nearer to perfection, nearer to the actual experience of a welling joy from within, and in that atmosphere of joy the individual is capable of working.

Anyone of you who has got a hobby can very easily understand this. When a man has got a hobby, he is working on it. Hobby means an activity of the hand and the legs, wherein your head and heart is concurring. When the hand is doing something wherein the head and the heart are also present, as in gardening, the man says that it is a recreation for him. Another man says playing cricket from morning till evening is a recreation for him. Yet another man playing tennis or football and sweating like hell, says it is recreation. If you are asked to sweat that much for doing a work for your neighbour, you say it is a museebhat. * But in spite of the amount of energy and perspiration spent in a tennis court or a football ground, you come away saying that you feel lovely.

The tennis player not only puts his physical effort, but also his head and heart while playing tennis. He has for the time being, forgotten all distractions of his mind, either of the past, or of the future or of the present. He is pouring himself into the sport, and yet he feels like a revived, rejuvenated young man. Similarly, from morning till evening we could have spent all our energies outside with our hands and legs, but if only we know the art of bringing our head and heart to the field where we are working with the hand, then we would have discovered that the longer the hours that we put in, the greater is the exhilaration and joy. Really speaking this is a wondrous joy indeed.

The so-called joy that you get from cinema is no joy at all. On a Sunday from twelve o'clock you are standing in the queue to get a ticket and the queue is long. You cannot expect a shamiana** all over the place to shelter the queue. Therefore you stand in the hot sun, and you ask anybody going along for a Coca-Cola so that you may not run the risk of losing your place in the queue. Standing there, perspiring, sweating,

---

* big trouble!
* a canopy

hungry, you at last get a ticket. You are very happy. With that ticket you go inside, and in the theatre you are supposed to find out very great excitement, because you are going to have your enjoyment. You go and sit down. But your mind is worried. Your physical body in the theatre is supposed to be enjoying the picture. But a thousand worries are there – tomorrow's problems and yesterday's regrets. When you come away from the theatre, you say the picture was very bad. The other fellow says: "What are you talking, fool? A very wonderful picture it is!" So, now two opinions!

You swallow the words and walk home and then you feel that the picture after all is no good at all. Thus, nowhere do you find enjoyment.

The real enjoyment is in the activity where your head and heart can come in. This activity you may find very exerting, boring and unhappy, but another individual enjoys it very vigorously. This is especially so in picnics. In summer vacations the South Indian boys go to the north for a holiday. They get down at Agra and walk along the roads, which appear deserted during the midday. The people of Agra are afraid of sunstroke. They are afraid that even when they open the window, they might get sunstroke. When they look out, they see these miraculous people called the South Indians, walking without any protection. How is it they are walking in the sun, they ask? They close their window with the assumption that the South of India is probably hotter and therefore these boys are walking as if it were comfortable. But the poor South Indians do not know that it is too hot. They are living in a realm of their own! They have come to Agra to enjoy and they know that however uncomfortable it is, it is comfort for them, because they have got a purpose, to enjoy the holiday, for which they have come. Thus, moving on picnic in the hottest sun, eating any food, sleeping in a railway station, catching any train, and suffering in many ways, they enjoy it all. For their heads and hearts are where their physical bodies are moving!

After he has reached South India, if his old grandfather were to ask him to get pa*n** from the street corner, the boy will complain that the sun is too hot! a betel leaf folded usually into the shape of a triangle filled with spices for eating. He forgets that when the thermometer was standing at 114° Fahrenheit he was walking five miles on the tarred road of Agra, but enjoying all the time. Here the thermometer is standing at 80° Fahrenheit and he does not want to go out to bring pan for the old man, because his head and heart are not there and therefore he feels miserable.

You and I feel disappointed and dejected in life, not because there is no work in the world. We are not

---

* a betel leaf folded usually into the shape of a triangle filled with spices for eating.

discovering for ourselves a work wherein not only the physical body but our head and heart can also be brought in, and he who can bring all these three aspects of personality in a field of activity, works on in an inspired manner. Inspired work not only brings out high production in his efficiency, but also gives a great dividend of joy to the worker himself. To work thus seems to be the very 'Art of living' that has been described in the Vedas, especially in the Gītā. This method of activity in the world outside, as a solution for the problem of man has been explained in the Gītā in its own language.

In the modern vocabulary, I explained to you that first we should discover a goal to draw inspiration from and stop all wastage of that inspiration in unintelligent regrets of the past or in equally unintelligent imagination of the future, or in the excitement of the present. Thus, if we work on in the world, with the head and the heart where the hand is working, the very work gains the stamp of great efficiency, and speed and the joy of work is ours.

31. YOU, ME AND GOD

(A dialogue between a visitor to the Sāndīpany Āśram and Parama Pujya Swamiji, during a session with devotees).

"Swamiji, I don't believe in God."

It was a young man, modern, tight pants, tobacco pipe stuck at the waist, trim thin moustache. He spoke English with an Americanised drawl, and was evidently one of our university products, with higher education abroad; sophisticated, to the point of his pointed toes.

Swamiji beamed. 'Excellent!' With a broad welcoming smile, nodding his head slowly, Swamiji continued: "That's fine. I like you. You are the man I have been waiting to meet. I like your outspokenness. You are intelligent and you think independently. You have the courage to speak out your conviction, straight from the shoulder, as they say. Now come, what kind of a God is it that you don't believe in?"

The young man, who had made his statement about his non-believing, with a little hesitation, probably at his own audacity at denying God before a Godman, was pleasantly surprised at Swamiji's cordial tone and benign smile, and, feeling encouraged, went on:

"This God, who sits above the clouds, and judges men, and dispenses favours and punishments by remote control, at his own sweet will, don't you think Swamiji, it is all hocus-pocus?"

Swamiji laughed. "Shake hands, young man. I am entirely with you. Now, we are two, together. I too, don't believe in that kind of God. But...Hmm, did you have breakfast before coming?"

"Yes, Swamiji."

"Well, what did you have for breakfast?"

"The usual things, porridge, toast, scrambled eggs, coffee....."

"Eggs, that's nice. Eggs! Now, where did the eggs come from, Rām, that's your name, isn't it?"

Rām, with his brows raised, feeling that Swamiji was leading up to something, said; "I don't exactly know, probably from one of those new poultry farms near Poona."

Swamiji: "I don't mean that. How are the eggs made? Do they grow in fields, or are they made in factories?"

"Simple. I think you are pulling my legs, but, all the same I'll answer you. Hens, of course. Hens lay eggs, you know!" Rām said with an air of flippancy. Nodding his head, up and down, thoughtfully. Swamiji continued: "I see, I see, so the eggs come from hens. Now where do the hens come from?"

Rām, an intelligent man, could see the 'Trap' he was being led into. He started saying: "Of course from..." Then, wide-eyed, looked at Swamiji silently. Swamiji smiled: "So, eggs come from hens, hens from eggs, which again come from other hens, and so on, ad-infinitum. Can you, Rām, say with any certainty, which was the first cause? Egg or hen? How and why?"

Swamiji now addressing all the devotees present, went on: "You see, God is not just a person or individual, sitting in a palace above the clouds, dispensing favours. It stands to reason that every effect must have had a cause prior to it. The watch you are wearing did not make itself. Your breakfast did not cook itself. There was a cause, in each case. That cause must have emerged from a previous cause. God is now the very first cause. The sole cause. The uncaused cause. There was no cause before Him. He is the oldest, the most ancient, He was before Time. The 'Sanātana', the 'Purānah'. This causation hunting is the favourite pastime of the evolving human intellect, trying to trace everything to it ultimate origin. That which is beyond the point, at which the intellect gets stalled, is GOD. The intellect cannot come to a conclusion as to the ultimate cause as in the age-old example of the hen and the egg. 'Thus far, no farther' is the limitation of the capacity of the human intellect."

Rām was flushed with excitement. He was thrilled. In a faltering voice he asked, 'there does seem to be something in what you say, Swamiji. Am I to understand that That is God?"

"That, which you now speak of as God, my boy, the Muslim calls Allah; the Christian refers to as 'My Father in Heaven'; the Parsee worships as 'Ahura Mazda'. These are a few of the different ways in which He or It is referred to, but all are referring to the same Supreme Principle: **the cause behind all causes**. The source of all that was, now is, and ever will be. The Vedas refer to it as Brahman, the Absolute, the Infinite. The truth is one. The wise speak of it variously."

"But, Swamiji, the description does not seem to be complete. Is that all that God is? How can one come to know Him?"

"Now, you are really getting somewhere! I have not 'described' God. He cannot be described. To define Him is to defile Him. What I pointed out only constitutes one way, one manner, of approaching the Truth. It is just one aspect. Now your second question,

"How can one come to know Him? "Know Him?" He cannot be 'known' as you know this table or this chair or your wife or your pipe. He is not an object of the intellect. He is the very Subject. Have you heard of the great disciple of the Kenopaniṣad who approached the master and enquired: "Revered Sir, what is it, directed by which the mind cognises objects, the eyes see, the ears hear and so on." The master cryptically answered: "It is the eye of the eye, the ear of the ear, the mind of the mind". In fact, it is the very subject that enables the eye to see, the ear to hear etc. It is not an object of the senses or the mind or the intellect. Hence, to answer your question, I have to tell you that you cannot make God an object of knowledge. An example will elucidate the idea. You are walking along a dark country road at night, occasionally illuminating your path with the aid of a battery torch; you want to know how the torch gives light; you unscrew the torch, you will not be able to see the battery cells as the battery cells cannot give light unless powered by the battery of cells. Similarly, the eyes, the ears, the mind and the intellect, all of which get their own power to function from the Life Principle, cannot understand it as an object. God is thus conceived of as the Life Principle, in everyone."

The audience sat spellbound listening to this exposition of a difficult Vedāntic Truth in an easy lucid style.

"Then Swamiji, you say that God or Truth is something abstract that cannot be seen or heard or touched or even thought of. Am I right?"

"You are very much right. In fact, God is all this and much more. The Bhagavad-gītā says: "Weapons cleave it not; fire burns it not; water wets it not; wind dries it not. This Self cannot be cut, nor burnt nor wetted nor dried. It is not material; it is not matter, understand."

"Why did you say, Self?"

"The Supreme, Life Principle, is also the Self in you, in me and in everybody. It is the innermost core of your personality. The popular misconception is that "Man is a body, with soul". That is not correct. The truth is "Man is the soul in a body". He is eternal. The role of the body is likened to a worn-out garment that is discarded by the wearer at his will. Now, the other members of the audience who had been listening with awe and reverence took the opportunity to clear their doubts.

"Swamiji, if God cannot be seen or thought of, is an abstraction, is there any significance in idol worship?"

"Of course, there is a lot of significance. When your dear son is in America, and you cannot see him whenever you want, do you or do you not get solace by looking at his photograph? You do know that the photo is not your son, but only a piece of paper with various tones of grey, but it reminds you of your beloved boy and his great love for you. So also, the idols in temples are to remind the devotees of the ideal, the Supreme. Since the human mind cannot conceive of a formless Supreme, God is conceived of in form as represented by an idol. To the earnest devotee, the idol appears as a living embodiment of his Lord and he goes into ecstasy at its sight. It is, however, necessary to remember that the idol is not God, but represents God."

"Why is it, Swamiji, that, as in Christianity or Islām, a particular day of the week is not earmarked in Hinduism for temple worship?"

At this question, Swamiji drew himself up, straightened and roared at the top of his voice; "Hinduism is not a part-time job!" He then explained at length that the aspiration to associate with divinity cannot be restricted to any particular time. "Have you heard of the schoolboy who said that earth is round on Sundays and flat on other days? So also, a man cannot be made to be divine on Sundays and devilish on all other days. (May be, most of us are that way)."

"So constant practice, frequent association with the good, etc. are needed. The temple visits and worship should elevate the mind of the seeker and help him to keep his mind on a higher plane. He should also take other steps to continue the purification of the mind at all times of the day, at home, in the office and at the market place."

"What is a pure mind, Swamiji?"

"A pure mind is one which is calm, free from agitation. Agitations are caused mainly by our likes, dislikes and desires. Desires spell disaster, fulfilled or frustrated. Mahatma Gandhi was very fond of the 'sthitaprajña' portion of the second chapter of the Bhagavad-gītā, in which the causes and consequences of desire are most graphically described. It is the ladder of fall:

"When a man thinks of objects, attachment for them arises, from attachment desire is born, from desire (unfulfilled) arises anger, from anger comes delusion, from delusion loss of memory, from loss of memory, the destruction of discrimination, from destruction of discrimination, he perishes."

Swamiji added: "The Lord also points out that the three great entrances to hell are lust, anger and greed."

One in the audience asked; "I have read a good deal Swamiji, I also have convictions. Yet, to put these values in practice is my problem."

Swamiji: "This was exactly Arjuna's problem. The Lord advised him, 'Recognize your real enemies. They are desire and anger, born of passionate nature, all devouring and sinful.' Knowing your enemies will enable you to destroy them. Knowing your weakness, you will make efforts to discard them. Once you locate a dead rat in your wardrobe, that was emitting odour, you will promptly pick it up by the tail and throw it as far away as possible."

"Our śāstras have laid down a clear-cut procedure. The threefold practice consists of śravaṇa, manana and nididhyāsana. Hearing is not 'in-one-ear -out-through-the-other'! It is attentive listening to discourses on our great scriptures (including reading them), contemplating on the ideas contained therein, and lastly meditation. Many people come and tell me that they have gone through the Gītā many times. I tell them "Let the Gītā go through you once at least. It will do you more good." Not just hearing or reading, but absorption of the great ideas contained therein, assimilating them, and living those values will alone produce radiance in the life of an individual. Proper understanding and correct attitudes are important. For example, we often meet the allegation that Hinduism is an out of the world religion meant only for the recluse. The spirit of Hinduism is not understood by those who say this. Wealth is not a taboo for the seeker, but the constant craving for wealth is. Property is not prohibited, but one is enjoined to use it in the service of society.

The Vedāntic concept of renunciation has nothing to do with 'have' or 'have-not', in a physical sense; it means the attitude of non-attachment. The classical example in our ancient lore is that of emperor Janaka, living in the luxury of a palace, but still considered as such a great saint and sage that great aspirants went to him for guidance!

If you ask me "How to start?" My answer is "Just start." "When?" "Now!"

"Today is the best day. A better day will not come."

"The greatest master who lived and worked for the cause of religion in India, Ādi Śaṅkara, has laid down the prescription:

"Bhagavad-gītā and Viṣṇu Sahasranāma are to be chanted; always the form of the Lord of Lakṣmi is to be meditated upon. The mind is to be led towards the company of the good; wealth is to be shared with the needy."

"Now, many people wait for their retirement to take to religion. They will never take to it, because they will have new problems on the way."

32. WHAT TO DO

(Swamiji's tips for effective study)

…. when you have your books

Vedānta is a science, and so it must be studied in a systematic way. Start reading Kindle Life. Even here, don't try to read through, it is not a novel or something of semi-heavy reading. These are books for the students to reflect upon, all by themselves. So don't read more than 5 to 10 pages a day. Read slowly, carefully noting all the ideas developed therein. This may take 20-30 minutes and always make it a point to read your scriptures after your morning bath, before the breakfast and work.

As you read thus, a lot of tiny doubts will arise in your mind; sometimes you may question the very logic of certain conclusions in what you read. Please note them down in a notebook, kept separate for this purpose. Clearly express your doubts. After having recorded your doubts, forget them and continue reading your daily quota of pages.

On the following Sunday, or any holiday when you have some spare time, please take up the notebook, and a pencil in hand. Start reading your own doubts collected during the week. You will find, surprisingly, that you can check off many of the doubts because you have the answers already with you. The week's reading has widened your vision.

May be, there are some questions to which you have not got the answer. Leave them alone. From Monday continue the regular programme of daily study, recording all doubts whenever they arise in your bosom. Repeat checking up all the backlog of unanswered doubts. By the time you come to the end of the book, you will find your questions are answered. If there are any unanswered, the next book will clear it.

Go slow. There is no hurry. Your independent thinking is of utmost importance. Don't blindly believe, question every statement, accept no action greater than your own understanding. Then alone, we can enter into the science of Vedānta, then alone our knowledge can enter us.

When you have finished revising Kindle Life, at its end there is a scheme of study recommended. Follow the series as suggested and read each book carefully and slowly, in small doses. It is a 2-3 years study of half an hour a day.

TRY, YOU CAN, YOU MUST.

(Swami Chinmayananda)

PUJYA SWAMI CHINMAYANANDAJI'S MESSAGE

Decide what you want:

-If you demand but a life of money and power, of sense pleasures and fleeting joys, seek not GOD and His help. Sweat, toil, strive and achieve.

> -But, if you demand a life of Peace and Love, of Self-control and Pure Bliss, seek Him and His Grace through study, prayer and meditation.

Kindle Life can help to "Learn-Live-Share"

-In this introductory book 'Kindle Life' for the study of Vedānta - the 'Science of Life' and 'Art of Living', Pujya Swamiji unfolds the topics in graded doses, in a lucid and non-technical style, with emphasis on the practical application of Vedānta to Life.

SCHEME OF STUDY

S.No.	Title of the Book	Dose Per day		No. of times
1.	Kindle Life	10	Pages	3
2.	Manual of Self Unfoldment	10	Pages	2
3.	Bhaja Govindam	4	Stanzas	2
4.	Tattva Bodha	5	Pages	2
5.	Ātma Bodha	3	Stanzas	2
6.	Vedānta Through Letters	10	Pages	2
7.	Art of Man Making (Gītā Talks)	12	Pages	3
8.	Vivekacūdāmaṇi (Stanzas: 1-200)	4	Stanzas	3
9.	Meditation and Life	1	Chapter	5
10.	Nārada Bhaktī Sūtra	5	Sutras	3
11.	Gītā Introduction	10	Pages	3
12.	We Must	10	Pages	5
13.	Sādhanā Pañcakam	1	Stanza	3
14.	Kenopaniṣad	2	Mantras	3
15.	Gītā Chapter 1, 2 & 3	3	Stanzas	3
16.	Vivekacūdāmaṇi (Stanzas: 201-300)	4	Stanzas	3
17.	Kaṭhopaniṣad	2	Mantras	3
18.	Dakṣināmūrti Stotram	2	Mantras	3
19.	Gītā Chapter 4, 5 & 6	3	Stanzas	3
20.	Upadeśa Sāram	2	Stanzas	3
21.	Īśāvasyopaniṣad	3	Mantras	3
22.	Gītā Chapter 7, 8 & 9	3	Stanzas	3
23.	Muṇḍakopaniṣad	2	Stanzas	3
24.	Gītā Chapter 10 & 11	3	Stanzas	3
25.	Kaivalyopaniṣad	2	Mantras	3
26.	Vivekacūdāmaṇi (Stanzas: 301-581)	4	Stanzas	3
27.	Puruṣa Sūktam	4	Mantras	3
28.	Gītā Chapter 12	3	Stanzas	3
29.	Taittirīyopaniṣad	2	Mantras	3
30.	Hymn to Badrināth	5	Stanzas	3

31.	Gītā Chapter 13,14 & 15	3	Stanzas	3
32.	Aitareyopaniṣad	3	Mantras	3
33.	Gītā Chapter 16 & 17	3	Stanzas	3
34.	Praśnopaniṣad	2	Mantras	4
35.	Gītā Chapter 18	3	Stanzas	3
36.	Revise Gītā Chapter 1 to 18	5	Stanzas	2
37.	Aṣṭavakra Gītā	3	Stanzas	2
38.	Māṇḍukya and Kārikā	2	Mantras	

and read this book as many times as you can.

TRANSLITERATION AND PRONUNCIATION GUIDE

ॐ	oṁ	home	ॐ	oṁ	Rome
अ	a	fun	ट	ṭa	touch
आ	ā	car	ठ	ṭha	ant-hill
इ	i	pin	ड	ḍa	duck
ई	ī	feet	ढ	ḍha	godhood
उ	u	put	ण	ṇa	thunder
ऊ	ū	pool	त	ta	(close to) think
ऋ	ṛ	rig	थ	tha	(close to) pathetic
ॠ	ṝ	(long r)	द	da	(close to) father
लृ	ḷ	*	ध	dha	(close to) breathe hard
ए	e	play	न	na	numb
ऐ	ai	high	प	pa	purse
ओ	o	over	फ	pha	sapphire
औ	au	cow	ब	ba	but
अं	aṁ	**	भ	bha	abhor
अः	aḥ	***	म	ma	mother
क	ka	kind	य	ya	young
ख	kha	blockhead	र	ra	run
ग	ga	gate	ल	la	luck
घ	gha	log-hut	व	va	virtue
ङ	ṅa	sing	श	śa	shove
च	ca	chunk	ष	ṣa	bushel
छ	cha	match	स	sa	sir
ज	ja	jug	ह	ha	house
झ	jha	hedgehog	ळ	(Note 1)	(close to) world
ञ	ña	bunch	क्ष	kṣa	worksheet
त्र	tra	three	ज्ञ	jña	*
ऽ	'	unpronounced अ (a)	ऽऽ	''	unpronounced आ (ā)

Note 1 : "l" itself is sometime used.   * No English equivalent
** Nasalisation of the preceding vowel.   *** Aspiration of preceding vowel